What people say about Nick and the
Invisible PowerPoint show…

Nick Looby is one of the best presenters I have ever come across, his relaxed and informal approach works well and he always makes me sit up, listen and smile. Nick is a joy to watch and whenever I hear him speak I always learn something and apply it immediately! The best thing that Nick does is make you question the way you do things and he always gets you thinking. Simply Brilliant!

Hayley Roy: Managing Director, ChairsGB.com

Nick's humorous, but to the point style will keep your feet on the ground and your hands in the air, grabbing the opportunities that his presentation will help you identify.

Paul Wearmouth: Speaker, Mentor & Coach, PaulWearmouth.com

The pace of business change today has never been faster and the competition is global. Everyone is looking for a technology silver bullet but it's so often the case of smart computers and dumb companies. Nick could be your answer. He totally understands your most important but complex asset, your people, and his technique can unleash their true potential to let engagement and productivity soar.

Mervyn Middleby: Head of Technology & Operations, Broadcast Industry

The messages were powerful, strong and rang bells to signal 'Oh that's what I do, I'll have to change that.'

Andy Kirk: Leicester Fire & Rescue

Nick's *Invisible PowerPoint* presentation is not only fantastically funny and witty, it is completely unique. Nick engages the audience and gives great snippets of practical information. Anyone having to deliver presentations as part of their role needs Nick before they deliver any more.

Natalie Emmerson: Primary Care UK

The content and quality of his presentations sit well with all styles and levels of management. You go away making immediate changes that last a life time.

Margaret Fleming: Fleming Marvellous

Nick is so enthusiastic and bursting with energy you just cannot help but feel positive about your own abilities. This is not just for formal business presentations. It helps you in daily interaction and communication with everybody you meet.

Colin Regan: Technology Development Specialist, Belfast

This is a truly inspiring, creative and motivational presentation concept and one I would highly recommend to anyone who would like to boost their presentation skills and confidence.

Jessica Lee: Founder, Star Well Being

Nick is able to deliver high quality training and information to help people promote and present themselves. He is fun to work with and can deliver results immediately.

Neil Mansell: Property Investor at www.neilmansell.com

The Invisible PowerPoint Show and the Art of Communicating to Win

Allowing YOU to shine with power, purpose and passion

Cover design and creation by Spaghetti Weston Ltd

(www.spaghettiweston.com)

Author photo by Peter Evans Photography

(www.peterevansphoto.com)

Edited by the hugely talented Molly Looby

ISBN 978-1-291-10557-5

For Molly, James and Louisa

You are what life is all about

Acknowledgements

A huge debt of gratitude is owed to all of those who have given me the opportunity to share my message with their teams, those who have allowed me to share their time on stage and all of those individuals who have added to my journey of communication discovery – the adventures continue.

Special thanks to: Mervyn, Mark, Colin, Margaret and Andy.

Contents

Prologue –

Prologue

This was the straw that broke the camel's back...

It is a Tuesday evening, the wind is blowing with attitude outside but the networking room is warm, too warm really but business is business and networking can be a fabulous way to build relationships and increase trade.

Tonight's presentation was about to begin; take your seats ladies and gentlemen. I sit towards the back, which is my way and wait expectantly, to be both educated and entertained.

Am I wrong to expect both education and entertainment from a guest presenter? I hope not, otherwise networking events up and down the country will struggle to fill their seats and entrepreneurial business will be the poorer because of it.

"I need to start my presentation with an apology. I ran out of time to prepare fully and when I realised what was required it was too late..."

A strange start, I thought, as we all knew about the guest speaker two weeks ago – did no one mention this to our expert? Oh dear, I will be extremely surprised if this is the finest display of presentation excellence ever witnessed.

In fact, I was surprised, but not in a good way...

After a bumbling introductory five minutes in which the audience could not have known what the point of the presentation was, it occurred to me that neither did the presenter.

Phrases such as "erm, hopefully you'll get something out of this" And "I didn't really read this before (referring to a number of bullet points on a pointless visual) I am reading this as we go" do little to inspire or fill an audience member with enthusiasm.

It gets worse...

Demonstration video that doesn't work, slides clearly from multiple, unconnected sources, tiny, tiny graphics that were nonsensical, examples that the presenter couldn't properly remember and a string of half-finished sentences such as...

"you can... you know..." and then he was off onto another point.

To top it all there was a mobile that went off, not once but a number of times – you guessed it, it was the presenter's mobile!

Well that's 25 minutes I am never going to see again – or am I?

Does any of this sound familiar? It is certainly not the first time I have witnessed these common traits in a performance – quite rare to have them all in a single dose admittedly, but far too regular in presentations across the globe.

One of the saddest things about all of this is that the presenter was actually an expert in his field and has worked with market leading brands on ground breaking technical advertising campaigns – but unfortunately, none of this 'gold' was shared among the audience, it was abysmal and we (I) had a rubbish time.

Why oh why did the magic remain hidden? What is it that prevents us from shinning when everything we need is either in our heads and ready to be communicated, or at our finger tips ready to be shared?

In an age where we are surrounded by communication technology, have instant access to all manner of information, and have come to rely on rapid and impactful sound bites of data, far too many of us are still unable to make our point and deliver our message in a way that encourages others to listen.

Well that's about to change...

A word of warning

This is no ordinary presentation book.

There is no point holding back and sparing the punches – I never want to sit through another presentation like that again and I am determined to change the world – one presentation at a time if I have to.

This is a book that deals with the real and the practical, a book that has its feet firmly planted on the ground. I will happily share with you the ingredients that make up a disastrous presentation banquet and why this leaves such a poor taste in the mouths of our audience.

Such as the management review presentation I viewed from the side-lines, which began with a promised 15 minutes of summary (this was the management's opportunity to share results, account stability and future plans with their staff). The 15 minutes became 45 and had all the content to realistically fill 5! The entire presentation was aimed at other managers and did not resonate in any way with the 100 members of staff in attendancewho showed their 'appreciation' by reading magazines, checking emails, playing on their iPhones and drifting off to sleep.

One of the most worrying things about this, is that the presenter believes he/she is doing a good job at 'getting through' their slot and no doubt feels pretty chuffed once the ordeal is over.

We will, of course, explore all those aspects that you can undertake to make your presentations shine every time you have the opportunity to perform. Everything you find in these pages will be embedded in the real world and will guide you in a very realistic waythrough the adventures of the presenting realm, and how to communicate to win.

Each chapter will deal with a specific area of presenting and communication. So if you like, you can dip in and out of the pages to explore some specifics, or you can read the book, as intended, from cover to (glorious) cover.

To maximise the accessibility of the material I have distilled the key messages and highlights at the end of every chapter so you can read the book in *turbo mode* to give yourself a 5 minute reminder of everything that our modern day adventures have in store.

1. Introduction – Invisible but Hugely Evident

Established corporations are aware of the need for their employees to present with passion and power; some of the more enlightened have policies and training in place to educate their teams accordingly. I need, however, to begin with an uncomfortable question – how many of these teams care or are driven enough to focus on the craft of delivering knockout presentations? How many of you can put your hand on your heart and say that you communicate like a pro? Aren't we all a little too busy to research, revise and rehearse our presentation to the sales team, the finance department or even the entire staff? Wouldn't we rather tick along and blame everyone else for a lack of ambition or poor concentration, rather than admit that our presentation could have been better?

During my research for this book I asked a large number of skilled people from distinguished companies the following two questions:

1. How many of you have ever been told your presentations are really bad?
2. How many of you (hand on heart) believe your presentations are really good?

In every case, only the occasional brave soul would admit to the first question, and sadly, only a handful of my audience have ever raised their hand to the second.

This tells me a number of useful things – your audience generally expect very little from your presentation and will generally be polite (while you are in earshot) about your performance. It also tells me, which is more worrying, that few presenters can be bothered to excel and perform at a standard they consider to be 'really good'.

Is this a training issue, an indication of how busy we are, or a reflection of our working ethos across the board? I believe it is a combination of all these things,and it goes a long way to explaining why 95% of all presentations leave their audience both disappointed and dissatisfied, if not downright annoyed that you have wasted their time.

I know a trainer who can charge in excess of £ 2,000 per day for his unique blend of psychology, NLP, stagecraft and performance techniques to train organisation leaders how to perfect their business pitching skills and with multi million pound contracts at stake for these organisations you can see why they are prepared to pay handsomely for these essential skills.

Let us assume that we don't have a spare £ 2,000 with which to employ the skills of a professional coach but that our presentations are still incredibly important to us. This, surely, is why you are reading this book and have made the investment in these pages; to improve, enhance and perfect your skills in this hugely important area and at a slightly more affordable price.

I am talking directly to the entrepreneur inside of you, that part of you that cares enough to make a massive difference to their business and their career. We are not in the enviable position to invest thousands of pounds in our presentation education, but we have the drive, the ambition, the passion to present with power and enthusiasm, to enthral our audiences so we can win more business, open more doors and have more of life's good stuff.

When I first fell in love with the idea of training real people to do amazing things with their lives, to step outside of their comfort zones and challenge the world, I knew that the opportunity of presenting to an audience would be the perfect place to start this amazing process.

To give a voice to this desire, I created the *Invisible PowerPoint* show – a 60 minute presentation based around that hugely popular (when I say popular, I mean 'widely used') piece of software created in the 1980's and developed for better or worse ever since.

The difference with the *Invisible PowerPoint* show is the fact that the 10 slides that hold all of the magic are, in fact, invisible, and this is just the start of a journey that is like no other.

60 minutes that will change the way you communicate, forever!

A bold claim indeed, but one that holds up with every audience I have ever had the pleasure of performing for.

For me, this has been the catalyst that has opened doors to a presentation world that is filled with the most amazing adventures and I would like to take this opportunity to thank all of those who have joined me on my travels so far – the voyage has been and continues to be humbling.

Throughout these pages I will show you how I create magic from the *invisible* and what components I rely on to educate, inspire and transform my audiences every time I have the opportunity and the honour, to present to them.

Summary Chapter 1 – *Invisible but Hugely Evident*

Just a brief summary to kick things off.

Opportunities for you to present are around every corner, if you want to find them. Your audiences expect very little (sadly) but you have the chance to make a massive impact and make your world that much more enjoyable, profitable and even more successful if you want it bad enough.

The key here is that you have to want it, we could all make do, but those who are hungry for more are those who tend to excel.

Work hard at your presentations and all of your communication opportunities so you and your audiences reap the benefits.

2. **From Invisible to Invaluable**

Presentation Outcomes

Education

Let's begin this chapter with a question – always a good way to begin any presentation, incidentally. The question I would like to ask is 'What would you consider a fabulous result for your presentation?' The reason I ask is the fact that the most powerful presentations differ greatly in their outcomes from those presentations that we are all too familiar with.

Imagine you have just rounded off your presentation and after a brief pause you hear the beginnings of what turns out to be a crescendo of applause rising into an ovation, your audience are on their feet and the applause echoes through the corridors and beyond – how rock and roll would that be? It would be like a theatre performance that builds to a rousing finish and has the audience on their feet in appreciation. Extremely rewarding but sadly, too rare in the *presentation* world.

Is that the outcome you desire? Let's face it, it would feel pretty good and would give the next person up to present something to worry about, but do we want more? Are we presenting only to educate and to entertain? If this is the case and applause is your audience's reaction, I think you have probably aced it so congratulations, enjoy the warm glow of success, job done.

This 'educating' presentation is the most common one I come across, although the rousing applause is shockingly rare. Mostly, they are of the type that set out to inform and instruct but typically do nothing more than leave us with the familiar feeling that we have just wasted our precious time. The phrase often prescribed to this waste of time is 'death by PowerPoint' – not a label you want attached to any of your work I assure you.

This is why I warn you against hiding behind your slides (if you are using any) and make sure you are able to share some of *your* knowledge, personality and stories with the audience.

The presenters that waste our time and feed us slides are never highly regarded. Because we are generally a polite audience, we wait until we have escaped from the room before we complain in whispers to our colleagues about them – we've all been there.

However, when this type of presentation is delivered well, it is like a breath of fresh air drifting through a meeting space and leaves the audience thinking that you are fabulous. Please resist the temptationto bow or go back for an encore, just be satisfied that you rock – but read on...

Most presentations are an opportunity to move your audience to even greater heights. Sounds a little out there and I'm not going to get all fluffy and begin preaching, but there are deeper levels that we *could* explore.

Inspiration

When you deliver your presentation well, if you entertain and succeed in winning the audience over, they will thank you for it –

they may not burst into spontaneous applause but they will ask you to present again.

I recently presented to a local networking group on the subject of *'After the Elevator,'* that little talked about but crucial moment when you've made your 'elevator pitch' and your audience says 'oh yes, that's interesting, tell me more...'

The subject was well targeted and the response was very encouraging, we all learnt a number of things along the way and I was consequently asked to present at another event – different subject, different audience, but another chapter in the presentation opportunity world and doors were opened and business followed – a good result.

So educating an audience is a fabulous and valuable place for our'communicating to win' opportunities to begin.

But, what if we could truly inspire our audience? Not only educate and entertain but also change their view of the information or subject of our presentation. Imagine the effect of the greatest films you have ever seen – those films that leave a lump in your throat and stun you into silence. Wow, now we are talking – 'It's an Incredible Life' or 'In Pursuit of Happyness', 'High School Musical'?, or any film that makes us change our behaviour and look at the world through new eyes. Inspirational to the point of thinking differently our perspective changes and great things can result.

These sorts of presentations are, admittedly, rare but can be done and <u>you</u> can do them, in fact you should be doing them.More of that later. These performances leave your audience not only thinking that you are fabulous, but also thinking that they are pretty great too, they are inspired and wonderful things can, and do follow.

I was at a local business promotional event recently and attended one such inspirational presentation. The audience were physically moved and were buzzing by the end of the performance. We were inspired to think more positively about our business and our lives – it was a good performance. When was the last time you can say a presentation made you buzz with appreciation? Not often enough I imagine.

There is, however, an even greater outcome that we can work towards and for some of your presentations this is where we should be aiming.

Transformation

It is one thing to encourage your audience to **think** differently but imagine if you could encourage your audience to **act** differently too.

Occasionally, someone will take to the stage or stand in a boardroom or even deliver a few words at a family function, and the effect will be memorably powerful. I have been fortunate enough to be at various examples of these presentations – people such as Topher Morrison, Christopher Howard and Dr. Joanna Martin take their audiences on a journey and amazing things can be achieved when you are professionally led along the path of discovery.

These audiences are instantly thinking 'what now' and their future actions are directed by your performance – incredibly powerful and those who can achieve such a response will find themselves indispensable. This really is the rock and roll of the presentation world.

I even attended a funeral recently where the eulogy was delivered with such passion, sincerity and poise that it went beyond reflection and celebration of a life well lived and had the audience thinking differently about their own lives to the point of taking action and seizing the moment.

I am not saying that every presentation you make should be nominated for an Oscar, but given the right opportunity, it would be incredible to engage your audience at this level. We will cover how we can stir your audience to action in our chapter about **Closure**.

So, we have a series of outcomes that will provide a frame upon which we can build our presentations. If we can educate and entertain, then our skills will be beyond most of those who have ever been asked to present, if we can exceed this level then there is a good chance our opportunities will be extraordinary.

Clear Powerful Communicators

We live in an ocean of global communication; Facebook, MSN, Twitter, Email, Texting, Blogs etc. Messages are everywhere in every format imaginable. We filter as best we can, but we are fighting a losing battle. When I was at school, if you were smart, you would know which book to consult to provide the right answers. Now, if you are shrewd, you know which words to feed into your search engine to narrow down the places in which your answers will be hiding.

Technology has, on the one hand made communication so much easier, but on the other hand it has opened us up to incredible challenges. How are we to take all of this information and communicate effectively to our audience? Now, more than ever before, the golden rule of **less is more** is to be heralded as our presentation mantra.

Too few of the presentation population are able to communicate succinctly, with the clarity that is desired in today's workplace. Our lives have become more complex, busier, and our time has never been so precious (ironic really considering the number of 'time saving' devices at our disposal). This has made way for those who can communicate in an understandable and clear way; these are the people worth investing in.

Those of us who can construct an email using normal language, rather than thesaurus-heavy formal text and can present using a conversational tone rather than management speak spread across a thousand bullet points, are those who will excel, both in the workplace, and beyond.

Imagine a sales person who saves you time and effort by clearly and rapidly summing up all the benefits of their product so you are able to make a decision to purchase (or not) on the spot,or a manager who can give his team all the necessary instruction and guidance in half the time of a normal Monday morning meeting. These are the stars of now, and will be shining bright as they guide us through these cluttered times.

I encourage you to adopt the lessons we are about to learn in these pages and promote yourself into a position of power by becoming a communications expert – read on and absorb.

Selling

It has long been said that nothing in business happens until something gets sold, and within reason this is mostly true. It is certainly true that without sales, a profitable business cannot exist.

When you make a sales presentation, you are in such a strong position to secure business that every aspect of your performance should be regarded as your best effort. What would you rather, four individual meetings with purchasing managers and their peers within your target client, or one presentation to the purchasing group as a whole? I know which one I would prefer, and I know which one is more likely to result in a purchasing decision being made. Get them all in a room, together, and present like a pro and you have all the makings of a successful sale. Take part in a number of differing meetings with differing members of the team and you have all the makings of a laboured process which is at the mercy of so many external factors you will have to work four times as hard to close the deal.

Sales presentations are commonplace – those who can perform exceptionally in these situations really bring home the bacon, for their company, for themselves, and even for their clients. More success in less time – it is difficult to put a value on that, but rest assured there is incredible significance in it and the following pages will enable you to harness this power and communicate to win. Read on.

The *Feet on the Ground* Approach

As a company, we are dedicated to improving lives. That sounds rather gallant and somewhat selfless doesn't it? However, we are dedicated to improving our lives too so we're not too selfless – we are a business and we work hard for our clients and we all reap the rewards of our success.

Our philosophy is very much in our name and we work in an extremely practical way, dealing with the processes that work. We look at life as an adventure and we love what we do. This is why I write with such passion about presentations, we not only train people to present, to communicate, to sell, but we use presentations throughout our businesses to promote, empower, invigorate, educate, entertain, inspire, and to transform.

Become a valuable presenter and excel at work, at play, and at things that you have not yet even considered.

Summary Chapter 2 – *From Invisible to Invaluable*

There are many forms of communication and in this day and age we are surrounded by a *noise* of information. If you can control this *clamour* and deliver clear, succinct detail and messages that are simple to understand and ideas that can be adopted instantly, then you will be a hugely valuable asset.

Those individuals who can master the skills of the modern, inspiring presenter will be the most valuable assets forward thinking businesses possess.

Excel at communicating and golden opportunities will be yours.

3. Planning Your Show

Map Reading for Beginners

They say that a journey of a thousand miles begins with a single step. That sounds fair but it's sure going to help if that first step is in the right direction.

Your presentation is a journey with a beginning, a middle and an end (just like a well told story) and it is your job to lead your audience in the right direction otherwise they will easily lose their way and end up in the wrong place.

Consider yourself the Sat Nav of the presentation world – you are in charge of directing your audience and just like the good old navigation system, you decide which route to take on your way. My Sat Nav does like to choose some peculiar routes though so it will also pay us to have an idea of the most effective route to take for our presentation journey.

Nothing wrong with peculiar routes I say, these are quite often the more memorable parts of the journey and certainly the parts of the journey that we tell our friends about – the single lane shortcut that has not seen traffic since Henry Ford took a wrong turn, or the little known cattle track that looks like a scene from an Indiana Jones film. For most presentations it is the 'peculiar route' that has the biggest impact.

It makes great sense though to have direction and purpose – ask any boy scout I am sure they will agree, so a road map is going to assist your audience and make sure we all stay on track.

So let's put together a simple process to make sure our audience arrive safe and sound and refreshed, ready to enjoy our chosen destination.

Mind the GAP

For those of you who have travelled on London's glorious tube system, this will ring a few bells. I use this well-known phrase to start our map building process and just like the 'mind the gap' warning on London's underground, this process will stop you and your audience falling down a dark hole which is not only dangerous, but will prove a struggle to climb out of.

The first thing we must consider when we have a presentation to deliver is the **G** of Gap which stands for **Goals**.

The goals are our destination, the end point of our journey and the ultimate decider as to how successful your presentation has been.

The first goal we must consider is '**what do we want to achieve for our audience**', this, after all, is why we are here presenting in the first place isn't it? What is it that we want our audience to derive from our time on stage? Imagine you are the tour guide and it is your responsibility to explore exactly what your audience would love to see and hear so that they gain maximum value from the experience.

More often than not, the main goal is one of information download or knowledge transference(*to educate*) – we know something that our audience need to know and it is our job to make sure, by the time the presentation is over, they know what we know and can retain this useful and required information. Simple huh? Well yes and no – if we're not careful we could leave our audience behind –

just like when you have friends following you in separate cars, if you don't regularly check your rear view mirror, you're not going to notice that they were stopped at the lights and are now lost, adrift in the Milton Keynes rush-hour.

How many times have you sat through a presentation and your journey began well, and with all good intentions you tried to keep up with the car infront, but for one reason or another your concentration dipped and you lost the plot, never to get back on board? Happens so often it is scary.

In business, our time is too precious to lose our way or take random trips to mystery destinations; we need reasons, timescales and destinations with purpose.

Why are we going there? When are we going? What are we going to do when we get there? What will it be like? Who will be there? How long will the journey be? How are we going to get there? Shall I pack a picnic?

Okay, without too many digressions we have opened up our **goal** and have a series of questions to ask on behalf of our audience.

So what is happening here? We have a journey to make and we need to ensure that our audience not only arrives at our chosen destination, but they need to arrive in good shape and in good spirits. Our communication **goal** is based on what we want them to draw from our journey, so it is only right that we put ourselves in their shoes and focus on what they need from us. For our presentation to be a success our audience will need to take on board our message and we will need to outline the benefits, **to them**, of this new information as we work through our show.

All audiences, whatever their size or motivation, are concerned by the benefits of the information we are able to deliver in our presentation, so make sure you climb insideyour audience's heads and explore what they would profit most from knowing. Before you have even opened your mouth your audience are sitting there wondering '**what's in it for me**'.

How many presentations have you been to where the value to be derived has not been clear at the start, in the middle and sadly, at the end?

I have been to countless 'performances' that are unclear about their goals and these are the shows that leave me most frustrated – there is a critical void that is never filled and the event is filed under the 'frustrating waste of time' category.

When I was at university, I weighed-up the merits of each lecture that was available and decided to attend (or not) based on how useful the information was likely to be. Business presentations don't tend to have this freedom of choice – we are expected to attend and too many deliver minimal value. If we had more choice I would imagine audience numbers would be as sparse as those in the university lecture hall. Something is wrong here surely!

By asking questions about our journey, we explore the aspects that will allow us to reach our audience most effectively. Too many presentations, sadly, are created upside down – consider this scenario:

I have a presentation to give on subject 'x'

No problem, I know lots about subject 'x'

Type, type, tap, tap, slide, slide, slide, slide, slide etc.

Dadah! Ready, let me at them...

Answer me this; good presentation or bad presentation? Difficult to know without being there. Audience focused presentation? Not on your nelly.

If we don't start the presentation process with our **goals** in mind, (our well thought out and <u>audience focused</u>**goals)** we and our audience are in for a whole host of pain – ours will be just like the 95% of all other presentations we have had the misfortune to sit through.

We run the risk of creating a presentation that is simply upside down - full of content but lacking direction. Sadly this type of presentation lacks the focus that our common sense tells us is an essential part of our communication process.

I actually can't think of anything that works well that has been constructed upside down (answers via email please to www.iknowupsidedowncoolstuff.com).

So please begin your presentation process at the top by asking yourself 'what would be a really awesome win for the audience if they left knowing...?'

For example, a presentation that sets out to 'increase your communication power to ensure you win more sales in less time' or a show that instructs an audience on the 'seven secrets of pain free investing' and encourages individuals to partner with your investment company, have a clearly defined direction and focus. As long as these are the topics your audience are interested in and the performance delivers on its promise, then your show will be filed in the 'thoroughly glad I went to that' category.

Talking of the audience, this brings me neatly to the second aspect of our *Mind the GAP* road map for presentations that deliver. The **A** from the word GAP stands for **Audience.**

Who on earth are they? What do we know about them? What do they really need to hear and what would really turn them off?

How many times has a presenter asked you what you want from their time on stage? It is a sad fact that far too often presentations are made without any clue as to what the audience *really* needs.

One of the first things we are looking to establish with our audience is **rapport**, and as we deliver our information we are looking to constantly create **empathy** – believe me this is so much easier when you know your audience.

I am not suggesting that you wait until you begin your presentation to ask your audience what they are looking for, although, that would be kind of interesting. But as part of your preparation you really should ask an audience representative or two (beforehand) what they would benefit most from.

"I am presenting to you and your team next week about how technology is changing the waywe approach our clients – you know the audience better than I do – what would really get them going and what would turn them off? Any thoughts?"

"Thanks for asking Nick, my team really hate PowerPoint slides, that's for sure – last week we had Dave in to present and it was a mass of slides, most of which were condescending – my guys simply turned off, what a waste of time. How about concentrating on your experience of how technology has helped you? Give them some real examples to work with – they are a practical bunch they would like that."

Suddenly we have the makings of a far more focused presentation and a much clearer view on what will and what won't work with this audience. Time to re-think the standard (pre-prepared) corporate presentation of 50 slides and come up with something that will hit the mark.

If at all possible, please seek out someone who can shine a light on what makes the audience tick, even if it's just to find out what they won't appreciate.

I have seen people re-working their old presentation – usually PowerPoint slides, usually in an airport departure lounge, usually in a real hurry with no consideration as to what the audience really want to hear. Does this ring any bells? Is this you?

I *overlooked* one such presentation construction recently that went from a title of 'BAA Service Review' to a 'new' presentation called 'Sky Meeting' while I was sipping latte in the departure lounge of Stansted Airport. While I was awaiting the first flight out to Belfast International, with a day of presenting and workshops ahead of me, presentation heartbreak was taking place before my eyes.

Now I would imagine that the audiences for these two presentations (BAA and Sky) differ quite a bit, but amazingly, only three of the slides were changed, some alteration in the bullet points and tweaking of titles and job done – close laptop, eat bagel, drink coffee.

How bad is that (I'm talking about me looking over this guy's shoulder, of course) an important sales presentation but no unique audience consideration. File this with the other 95% of 'I don't care enough' presentations. Hands up all those who are guilty of this though? Just wanting to get the job done and out of the way so we can move on and focus on what's going on in our world.

If this is you then it's simply not good enough – we all know it and we have all sat through enough poorly targeted presentations to know that an increase in quality is essential. If we want to **communicate to win** then we need to up our game.

We must create empathy with our audience if our message is to be taken to heart and if we're not careful we are going to be wasting everyone's precious time, including our own.

"No one cares how much you know until they know how much you care"

Don Swartz

Do yourself (and your listeners) a huge favour and explore what is going to work with *this* audience.

So rare is this focused, targeted and fit for purposecommunication that audiences cannot help but be transfixed from the start. You will find this audience will appreciate everything they see and hear and if the truth be told, they would probably be happy to pay for the pleasure(ask any entrepreneur if they have paid to hear the best presenters and I can guarantee a huge proportion of them will have) – makes you think doesn't it?

So we have **G**oals and **A**udience from our *Mind the GAP* process and it is at this point and <u>**only**</u> at this point, that we should be **P**reparing our presentation. If you can master the **G** and the **A**,then you are ready to put together a presentation that is likely to hit the mark and deliver excellent value for your audience.

Let's explore in a little depth how best to put our presentation together – let's get into the *construction* business...

Summary Chapter 3 – *Planning your show*

Don't bore the pants off your audience!

Put your presentation together in a way that works for you **and** for your audience. Use the *Mind the GAP* process to focus on the **goals** that will work for your listeners. Consider who your **audience** are and ask them (as best as possible) what will work for them and use this information to prepare your show. This way you can construct something that will build empathy and rapport and be of real value to your observers.

4. Construction

Now that we have a solid plan based on clear goals and our knowledge of what makes our audience tick, we can begin to **P**repare our presentation; a presentation that will now be focused on the needs of our audience and will engage on their level.

As with most communication skills, this one is not rocket science and we can keep the process pretty simple. All we need to be able to do is to ask ourselves a few standard questions and we will have the keys to creative, powerful presentation construction.

- What are my three core messages and why are these important – what benefits will they bring my audience and will we need to break these down?
- What is the best way to put these messages across to **this** particular audience?
- How long do I have to get my message across?
- What stories can I use to communicate the message to maximum effect?
- What shape should I use for my presentation?

Let's take a brief look at these questions in turn...

What are my three core messages and why are these important?

There is no point trying to squeeze more than three main points into your presentation, as your audience, bless them, can only take in so much information – in fact, even with three main points you are going to have to structure your information clearly for the messages to stick.

I need to communicate A, B and C; now ask yourself why. WHY??? This way we can begin to explore the benefits this information will bring the audience – don't forget they are thinking 'what's in it for me' before you have even begun to present. Think of the **why** and you are on the right track. As mentioned earlier, we are looking to establish empathy with our audience, so put yourself in their shoes and consider what would really work for them. Ask yourself 'if it was me in the audience I would like to hear...' this should shine a light on what our main messages need to be.

Always communicate your message in terms of the **<u>benefits</u>** for the audience – they love that, highlight the good stuff; even a presentation that is communicating bad news can look to solutions rather than dwell on the negative.

Add value to your audience; give them **your** magic in a form that they can take away with them, so they are able to depart much better off from their presentation experience.

Consider the *invisible* aspect of **your** show – the magic that emanates directly from you and doesn't rely on slides, bullet points, graphs, charts or any other visual – what do **you** have that will engage your audience in a way that leaves them wanting more?

If you were in your local pub, sharing an interesting and informative story with some friends, you would be relying on this 'stand-alone' expertise and your friends would experience the real you. Give your audience a glimpse of this *gold* too.

What is the best way to put these messages across to this particular audience?

When the sales and marketing teams of the BBC's department I was working for were being made redundant (announced in one hugely anticipated presentation) the manager with the unenviable task of breaking the news began the presentation with the following enquiry –

"I have a set of PowerPoint slides with all of the information on or if you prefer I will simply tell you what is going on and answer your questions".

Can you guess what option the audience went for? You bet; they went for the no nonsense 'talk to us and answer our questions' approach. The manager in question could see the human side of the situation and knew his audience well enough to deliver the information in the most appropriate fashion. I was in that audience and, although my contract was coming to an end anyway, I quite enjoyed it – I do see life as a whole set of adventures though and opportunities such as this one really get the pulse racing – bring it on I say!

If you know your audience you can apply your common sense and consider the best vehicle for delivering your information. Sometimes this will be through a set of stories that transport your ideas into the minds of the audience; sometimes putting information onto slides will be effective, but don't fall into the extremely common trap of trying to present a hand-out (lots more about how to use and not use PowerPoint later).

For example, a presentation focusing on the three main reasons why road safety should be reviewed, would be radically different if it was being delivered to the local county council or the nearest 6th form college – different audiences look for different things, so be aware of how yours tick and make sure your delivery has high impact and adds value on their level.

If I am delivering my *Invisible PowerPoint* show to a group of entrepreneurs at a networking meeting, my performance differs greatly to the same show delivered to a group of managers from Network Rail for example. The needs of both audiences are similar but the drive behind these needs is radically different. Those who run their own business tend to hunger for presentation hints and tips to enable them to close more sales, win more pitches and increase their revenue. Management teams from blue chip companies are looking for clear communication skills to impart information succinctly and in a way which will label them as a serious player within the organisation, in turn enhancing their internal career prospects.

How long do I have to get my message across?

Most presenters are given an hour to deliver their messages (45 minutes of presentation and time for questions) but far too often that hour slides and the goal posts are moved beyond your control.

Have you ever been to a presentation where the presenter is running behind schedule or is taking longer than planned to deliver? It happens all the time and usually you are up next and your 1 hour slot has become 35 minutes – bugger!

If you are given an hour then by all means prepare for the hour – don't forget to rehearse out loud (more of this later) to make sure that it is actually an hour but also consider what you can deliver in 30 minutes or less. If you really know your material this should be fairly straight forward. If you rely heavily on PowerPoint slides and have masses of information, this is going to be far more difficult – audiences will not thank you for whizzing through slides in a desperate attempt to squish everything in to a reduced time slot.

The *invisible PowerPoint* doesn't rely heavily on slides to deliver the value – it's the knowledge and experience you have that ultimately counts.

Be realistic and consider the key messages and deliver these in the time available – sounds easy huh but you really need to be comfortable with your material to change the structure at a moment's notice.

I went to a networking event recently at which you are given 60 seconds to talk about who you are and what you do. I had fine-tuned my 60 seconds of self-promotion so it was totally on the money, not a second more, not a second less, only to be told as we were about to begin the round of 60 seconds that, due to time constraints, we would only have 20 seconds each to speak. What to do? Deep breath and go for 60 seconds at triple speed? I don't think so. Key message, keep it simple, don't rush and make it memorable.

It pays to think ahead and have your 'plan B' ready and available, an edited, value filled view of your information which can be adjusted to fit within any time constraints that are applied.

Think of this as the 'mercury' version of your show which (like the liquid metal) can mould itself into the available space and fill it with something that can read the temperature (of the audience) perfectly.

What stories can I use to communicate the message to maximum effect?

They do say that 'Facts tell and Stories sell' – 'they' seem to know what they are talking about so let's have a think about our stories, after all, these are the things that are usually remembered most by your audience.

Stories make presentations come alive and add the much needed human aspect to many a diatribe of information overload. (Much more on this in chapter 11).

Christopher Howard, a great presenter and NLP guru, says that the main reason for telling stories is to bypass the audience's conscious resistance to hearing the point that is being made, and we know that throughout history stories have been used, to amazing effect, to transform ideas into reality.

So let's transport our information into the minds of our audience by telling stories.

Imagine we have an important point to get across to our audience such as:

"Before we present we should get to know our audience as thoroughly as possible"

We want this message to sink in and stick so we back this information up by telling a story.

The story I would use dates back to my early days in sales in the broadcasting industry. My Management team were invited to attend the monthly board meeting of a very well-known independent production company to discuss collaborative working

– oh my they walked into a scene that resembled the ending of Butch Cassidy & the Sundance Kid, with similar results too – it was awesome – but then again I was only observing.

Although I had forged the relationship with the production company and set up the meeting opportunity (no sour grapes, honest), my management team at the time thought this was an opportunity not to be missed and stepped in to steal the limelight and (potentially) to create a stronger working relationship with the other company.

Little did we know (because we didn't understand our audience and their motivations) that the reason for allowing us into the board meeting was to unleash a tirade of abuse in our direction concerning shared franchise opportunities and the company's restrictions to turn a shared brand into a money making machine.

It was quite simply stunning and taught me the valuable lesson of understanding your audience in depth and in detail.

So with this example I have a story to back up an important point – the story itself is engaging and interesting and could stand alone with most audiences, but here we use its power to drive the point home about the importance of understanding our audience's needs before we open our mouths.

As it turns out, the Management team walked into a storm which they should have seen coming, but simply didn't think ahead or provide their (our) audience with the courtesy of understanding their position and concerns. Be warned...

With stories we can really engage; they don't even have to be our stories but ones that will resonate with our audience – for example, 'I heard a story the other day about blah blahblah and what happened was blah blahblah and this reminded me that in our business we use the exact same approach to our customer service strategy and this has to change' (I am assuming you put your own details in place of the 'blah, blah, blahs' otherwise your story is going to fall flllaaaaaat).

With some consideration of who the audience are, you can put together your list of stories that will strike a chord, add value to your messages and enhance the way you communicate.

Please make sure that your stories have a suitable purpose, otherwise you will simply be providing a distraction for your listeners – stories without a point are like darts without a flight – they travel but usually end up bouncing onto the floor and not scoring any points.

Try telling success stories, audiences love these, nothing sells like success does; psychologically, your audience will be looking for positive outcomes to your stories.

Always worth practicing the story too – know your meaning, the sequence of events, and work on your delivery – just like with the finest comedians, sometimes the timing is crucial to creating the right impact.

What shape should I use for my presentation?

What are you talking about Nick? Well, psychologically, audiences like to follow patterns; it keeps the content on track, providing more digestible information. Patterns are sometimes critical for assigning meaning and influence how we interpret messages.

Presentations entitled '3 Ways to Earn More with Less Effort' or for longer sessions 'The 7 Steps to Financial Freedom' are following a list format (pattern). Members of the clergy tend to use patterns based on a single word for example 'SIN' what this really means – they then work through the letters of S.I.N which all stand for a key point, for example **S**inister, **I**mmorality and **N**egligence. The audiences (especially the spectacular sinners) can follow this pattern and psychologically the information is easier to grasp – the presentation road map is set.

Whatever the pattern you decide to work with, it needs to be obvious for your audience and it makes sense to choose a pattern that appeals to the entire room – no point picking the formation and shape of a football team as a pattern to present your company sales strategy if your audience can't even fathom the off-side rule.

Pick wisely and your information will be easier to digest and is therefore far more likely to sink in to your audience which, of course, is a major factor in deciding if your presentation journey is a huge success.

Summary Chapter 4 – *Construction*

Don't overload your audience; deliver your 3 key points (no more if you can help it) and ensure the benefits are obvious.

Your audience are thinking *what's in it for me,* so focus on their needs. Consider what you would like to hear if you were receiving the show.

Ensure you are prepared for the time available, even if the time is cut in half with minimal notice. Know your material, back to front, front to back and inside out.

Have stories ready to back up your key messages and consider if your show would benefit from a particular pattern or shape.

5.Kapow! The Big Opening

'*HAERSMDCIT*' doesn't mean a great deal to most folk I come across – my kids know what it means but they are in the minority for sure. I like it, it makes me smile and strangely, now I've got used to it, I find it most helpful.

Don't panic though, this is not the start of an acronym highway with corporate lingo broken down into unmemorable letter clusters.

What we are talking about here are the big 5 – the five things we should be looking to do to engage with our audience from the moment we appear on stage.

First impressions count in the world of communication – no doubt about it. We are increasingly judged on first impressions in so many parts of our fast paced, time poor life that we need to be sure about the impression we give in everything we do.

It is so difficult to recover from a poor first impression, ask anyone who has spilt their coffee at a crucial job interview or has turned up at a first date wearing white socks. So time spent on our '*big opening*' is time very well spent.

Unless we all have some hidden magic that will soon be unleashed to wow our crowd (in the style of Britain's got Talent or the X Factor) we'd better make sure that first impression moment is as sparkling as it can be.

As we have already established, your audience, before they have even taken their seats, are thinking '**what's in it for me?**' and it's our job to hook them instantly.

Consider this the welcoming handshake with which we will open our audience to our content, our presentation style, our story, and our whole reason for standing tall in front of the eager masses. That 'introductory handshake' needs to be firm in a *welcome to our club* kind of way as opposed to a wet, *I'm petrified of you*, lettuce hand quiver.

We need to achieve a number of essential things in our opening and we can't hang about – so let's get to it.

Making HAERSMDCIT Visible

HA   We need to **H**ook our **A**udience first and foremost –

BANG!

We need your attention, this is it, we're up and running and it's going to be awesome.

Before you catch any fish, you need to hook them. There is no point working hard to land a big fish if you haven't hooked it in the first place. We need a method of drawing attention and engaging our listeners immediately.

You can begin with a shocking statement, use a prop, make a strange and confusing declaration,get everyone on their feet, or ride in on a unicycle juggling with chainsaws – add some drama (maybe not this much but it would certainly get my attention).

I like to begin slightly less dramatically than the unicycling chainsaw fan; I can juggle with lemons but that is about the limit of my circus skills. I tend to begin by asking some questions to encourage interactivity with hands raised and some feedback or banter.

Whatever method you choose, you must ensure your audience sit up and take notice – hook – hook – hook 'em.

At a networking event recently, I was speaking on the subject of Body Language and I began with the warning *"you can run, but you cannot hide..."* which definitely raised an eyebrow or two and I had them – nothing like a mild threat to get people's attention.

ER   We must also **E**stablish **R**apport with our audience. Create that 'one of us' feeling, share some common experience, get the audience on your level – people love to hear information related to what they do.   Give this some thought as you build your presentation, otherwise you will end up talking about the weather or the traffic on the local one-way system.

Acknowledge what the audience is feeling, be human and consider how you would feel if you were one of the listeners. Not only do we need the audience's ear, but we need them to buy in to us. Show them that you are worth listening to.

In my *Invisible PowerPoint* show, which explores the role **you** play in a *PowerPoint* presentation (and it is, of course, a major role) I ask the audience if they are fans of *PowerPoint*, to which the response is predictably groan filled. I then agree whole heartedly with them, that usually, *PowerPoint* means mind-numbing tedium.   Rapport established – we all agree – and then they are all ears.

SM   **S**etting the **M**ood is our next task. Give them a glimpse of what the rest of the presentation will be like and highlight the benefits (to them) of what you are going to say. We want the audience to say YES to our message and the style in which that message will be conveyed. For those of you who have been to my *Invisible PowerPoint* show, you will remember that I promise to revolutionise your view on using PowerPoint, and also deliver a set of tools you can instantly use to make every presentation you ever make engage and sparkle. I then ask if you are up for this – so far the response has always been a hearty 'oh yes please Nick' so we set the expectation and the mood of the room very early on. I allow my passion about my topic to flow through the audience.

Some audiences need more of a warming up than others, but if they can see the value in what you have for them, then you are half way there to having an engaged and interested throng.

DC Why should we listen to you Nick? How can you deliver these wonderful things that you promise? It wouldn't surprise me if my audiences are contemplating these types of questions.

Early on in your presentation the audiencemay not know who you are or how you are qualified to impart these gems of information. So we need to **D**emonstrate our **C**redibility and let the group know why our information should be regarded as worthy of ear time. It is only fair, that if we are asking the audience to say YES to our presentation, we should make this easy for them and give them good reason why we are worth listening to. Once again, give them the benefits (to them) of what your experience means. You know your stuff, which in turn will allow your audience to gain – don't forget they are thinking 'what's in it for me?' and you are *communicating to win* so highlight the important aspects that will highlight your value from their point of view.

IT   The benefits of our presentation should be leading the way when we entice the audience with our topic – we should speak in terms of what value our audience will derive from their time with us.

Consider this as an essential part ofIntroducingyour Topic, our 5th task while opening our presentation and opening our audience.

Introductions that simply state 'Tax changes for all SMEs for the new financial year' are less engaging than the same presentation that is introduced as 'No more HMRC headaches – making business simpler'. Instantly the audience can see the benefits of 'no more headaches' and a 'simpler' business which is far more likely to engage them than the simple 'statement' style of topictitle which we all see again and again especially when the presentation that follows is heavily reliant on *PowerPoint*.

So we have 5 tasks to complete in the first 30 seconds – 2 minutes of our presentation (it really does need to be that quick and focused). Apply HAERSMDCIT to your opening process and you can't go far wrong (bet the acronym is growing on you by now). Another way of remembering this (thankfully) is with the mnemonic 'Hungry Audiences Easily Reject Set Menus so Deliver Creative Inspiring Treats. Whichever way you choose to remember this, there is no escaping from the fact that the opening of your presentation is key to the success of your performance.

Summary Chapter 5 – *Kapow! The big opening*

Open your show like a pro and create a hunger for what you have in store for your audience.

Hook – make them sit up and take notice – open with a bang!

Rapport – put yourself in the audience's shoes and create that 'one of us' feeling.

Set the Mood – this is what the show will look like – give them a flavour of your magic.

Credibility – demonstrate why you are worth listening to, no need to brag but give suitable evidence to prove why you are the expert.

Introduction – highlight the benefits of what's in store, don't miss this opportunity to engage and create rapport.

Lots to cover and some key features to include in the opening minutes of your show – make it powerful and open the audience's ears.

6. Taming the Teenage Spiders

One of my main concerns about technology is that there is a tendency to rely on it to create our presentation impact. If we use our technology to deliver a *whizz-bang* impression it is bound to take the emphasis from us as the presenter and that is a dangerous place to be.

It's very difficult to build the essential rapport an audience needs ifour presentations relyheavily on screen based information – it is incredibly rare to build rapport with a film or a TV show after all.

During the *Invisible PowerPoint Show* we shift the emphasis away from the slides; in fact, our first *Golden Rule*(from the 6 that are contained in the invisible slides that I use) is that **You are your presentation and not your slides** (more about this later) so if we rely less on our technology, we need to put more emphasis on ourselves and that means body language (or as I call it 'taming the teenage spiders) so let's move it move it move it and make our presentations more physical and more memorable.

As we have already mentioned, audiences form their impressions very quickly indeed, so our appearance and our presence on stage are critical from the moment we appear. Don't forget to stand tall, be yourself and allow your authority to fill the room.

This is really important and shouldn't simply be a throwaway line – make sure you are standing straight, hold your head high, move into position in readiness to deliver your opening, pause, look at your audience before you begin, and then, when you are ready, go for it.

There are a number of scary things that came out of the 1970's, and the following statistics are no exception, so just in case you haven't come across these figures before, I will mention them now – the stats say that what audiences remember from presentations and our face to face interactions breaks down as follows:

55% of everything that an audience remembers in a presentation is based on what they see – but that doesn't include your bullet points (apologies to all the PowerPoint fans out there but we're going to have to do something more than talk through our slides).

38% of everything that an audience remembers from your performance is based on the tone of voice used – how you say your stuff is so important – it's one of the reasons Richard Burton could fill the Royal Albert Hall and enthral audiences by simply reading from a phone directory.

7% of everything an audience will remember from your presentation is based on your content. Only 7%! That seems a bit daft to me but these stats have been round the block and are generally acknowledged to be correct. 7%! Surely the content is the most important thing? You know what, it is essential, as a presentation without content is as useful as an electric kettle without a plug. But, if you don't work on the other two aspects your presentation is going in one ear and out the next and simply won't be remembered the way we hope it will. Over 90% of your impact does not have anything to do with the content you so diligently crafted, so we need to do something slightly more than regurgitate our (in some cases) impressive knowledge.

The answer (in the words of Olivia Newton-John) is to get *physical* with your audiences.

The key to enhancing every interaction you will ever have and the answer to more impact, more sales, more success, and potentially the ability to read minds, lies in mastering the use and understanding of body language – let's explore...

Cheese!

First and foremost let's **smile** out there. Lower stress and achieve more positive outcomes with smiles. People like to do business with people who smile, allow your inner enthusiasm out though your genuine smiles and win more clients, close more deals and make people wonder what you've been up to.

From time to time I will have a *smile day*, during which I try to smile at as many people as possible (without looking insane – now that's the challenge).

Science tells us that a smile actually improves the mood of both the smiler and the smilee (I know I am making up words here but you get my drift). Sales experts tell us that you can hear a smile over the phone and listeners benefit from the 'smiling' conversation.

Unless your presentation requires you to impart really bad news, a smile sure isn't going to hurt anyone and can work wonders for creating rapport. Try it and see the results instantly – go on try it now and see how it feels. I am writing this chapter on a tube train which is one of the only places a smile is not appreciated – getting a few strange looks – I wonder if I could clear the carriage by smiles alone?

So it would be crazy, surely, to go against the latest science. Scientific proof suggests if we are happy we tend to smile – yep, I can buy that – of course. Stranger is the proof that exists that shows smiling can actually make us feel happy – if we feel a little out of sorts the answer is to force a smile (a kind of 'fake it 'til you make it, Anthony Robbins style) and psychologically our mood will lift.

Be warned, however, genuine smiles spread to the eyes and the fake ones don't even come close. This 'fake' smile can easily be read by your observant audience so be sincere. You can also use this information when reading the body language of others to give you the head's up when in conversation with a client or colleague who is smiling back at you.

It's surprising what we can achieve when our mood is right so *smiling* is both an obvious and an extremely valuable tool, if not an incredible one, so give it your best and smile. This is exactly why *Starbucks* have the message:

> "Smile, you are about to walk on stage"

posted on the doors that separate the kitchen area from the serving zone.

You looking at me?

The **eyes** have it. If you work on only two aspects of body language it has to be smiles and eyes – and it is so simple too. Eye contact is essential as it is the vehicle with which we convey our honesty to our audience. To ensure your listeners remain engaged with your story, work on regular eye contact – just a few seconds per person is fine, no need to stare. Generally in a larger group, if you allow your eye contact to linger with an individual those either side of that person will register the eye contact as their own – auseful three birds with one stone kind of arrangement.

The excellent book "Flipnosis" by Kevin Dutton, goes into detail regarding the power of eye contact and how this is an integral component of creating empathy. As this is an essential part of our communicating to win strategy,we must work hard with our eye contact to infuse our audience with our wise words and important messages.

Dutton explains that peacekeeping forces in Iraq find that those who wear sunglasses – therefore obstructing that key eye contact opportunity – report higher incidences of unrest and as a result, incur more casualties than those who keep their eyes visible.

Those who avoid eye contact are, not surprisingly, considered with some reservation – 'look me in the eye and say that' is often that gauge we use to assess the truth of a situation, so avoiding the eyes of our audience is not a wise move.

I can't remember seeing anyone present wearing sunglasses, although it may be quite cool to try – no that would feel weird and I am no way near American enough to pull it off, but the lack of shades on stage goes some way to show the importance of seeing the whites of theeyes.

You may get away with hiding your eyes around the poker table, but when in front of an audience who you want on your side, give them plenty of eyeball. After all, the audience are the ones who will give you the standing ovation if you wow them with your magic, so devote your attention to them and nothing else.

The eyes will also give you essential information as to what's going on in the heads of your audience.

Body language is a two way street and everyone is always communicating in some way through the language of body talk.

In a large group you can easily tell if your listeners are following, if they remain engaged and on message simply by the eye contact they are giving you. If their eyes drift away and you see signs that they may be losing interest, or even struggling to keep up with your delivery, then that is your cue to do something differently – try asking some questions, gather opinion as to how the information is going down so far, be human about it and encourage active participation to bring the audience back on to your track.

Watching for the eye contact (or lack of it) is a superb temperature check for how well you are doing.

During one of my *Invisible PowerPoint* deliveries, I noticed that one member of the audience was distracted, they kept looking at their phone and seemed more interested in whatever was going on with their mobile than with the topic being presented. The rest of the group were engaged and attention was extremely healthy. I decided to leave the single distracted member of the audience alone (sometimes it is not a great idea to explore what is going on behind the scenes) but at least I noticed and I could have chosen to change the pace, taken a pause and asked a few questions of the group if I'd noticed an increase in distraction.

As it turns out, the lady in question, came up to me at the end of the 'show' and explained that she was making notes on her mobile and was at pains to ensure I didn't think she was being rude, she was listening intently – bless the effective use of mobile technology.

In a smaller group or in a one to one scenario, you can pay far more attention to what is going on with the eyes, and far more information can be gleaned from what the eyes are saying.

Although not an exact science, body language will give us strong clues as to what is going on 'behind closed doors' and will direct us to what is not being said in any given scenario.

You can tell a great deal of what is potentially going on by careful observation of where the eyes are pointing at any point in conversation. Although not a guarantee, these indications are a general pointer as to what may be going on inside the head of others.

Top Right   There is a tendency for those who look up to theirright to be creating visual images (using their imagination), in some cases this will be an indication that they are possibly making stuff up.

One of my workshop delegates recently reported that he can now tell if his young son is lying to him when he questions him about his behaviour and actions simply by watching where his eyes travel to during the conversation – a success in anyone's book.

Top Left   If you are talking to someone who looks up to their left,this generally indicates that they are recalling visual images (searching their memory), in other words picturing things that have actually happened.

A recent delegate in one of my workshops was recalling what his IT team generally wear to work and his constant eye movement's to the top left indicated he could see them in his head and was using these images to recall the detailed information.

Try this out when you are next deep in conversation or observing an interaction or watch yourself in a mirror and see where your eyes go when you are recalling images and when you are making things up.

Bottom Right When the eyes look to the bottom right, this potentially indicates that the speaker is thinking about feelings and emotional aspects of the conversation.

Bottom Left Eyes travelling to the bottom left represents an internal dialogue taking place; we tend to do this when we are carefully considering our options.

If nothing else, these possible giveaways allow us to investigate further and dig a little deeper, by asking some exploratory questions we can see if what is being said is actually in keeping with what the body is telling us.

Move it move it move it...

There is something rather magical about a presentation that embraces powerful and purposeful movement. We are not talking about the kind of caged tiger style of pacing from left to right (I see this all the time) which is more of a distraction and gives off a sense of uncertainty and procrastination, but movement with purpose.

Use the complete space at your disposal – take a trip to the left of the stage (or presentation area) and make a point or two, head on over to the other side of the stage and make another point or two, and when you have your most important messages to deliver, head for front and centre of the stage where you will have maximum impact at this 'power position'.

Be definite about your movement, don't shuffle, take positive steps, and when you arrive at your chosen spot stop. Stay still.

Deliver your message before you move again. Positive, powerful movements which add value to your words – that's what we (and your audience) are looking for.

In some presentation spaces you will be able to move throughout the audience area. I recently presented in a showcase cinema and was able to move up between the rows of seats and occasionally engage my audience from a whole new angle – this is quite rare in the presentation world (it is rare to be presenting from a space that will allow such movement).

Topher Morrison is a great advocate of this type of freedom of movement as he regularly gets stuck in among his audience members, moving regularly around the room and even sitting down with particular individuals – this certainly keeps you on your toes and creates a familiar sense of rapport throughout the space.

Try to avoid movement that doesn't add vigour or energy to your routine. Rocking backwards and forwards, rolling onto the outsides of your shoes and shuffling about on the spot doesn't really make for a commanding performance. Think about the space you have available and build in some powerful moves.

If you have the opportunity to review the space within which you are to present, you can explore the movement opportunities you will have – try and build these into your show in the early presentation preparation process – it will make a massive difference.

Put 'em Up – control those spiders

Another thing to consider when building your presentation is (are) gestures. It is so obvious when a presenter doesn't quite know what to do with their hands, and that's when the fidgeting begins – mighty distracting I can tell you. As a wise man once said:

"Presenters who do not know what to do with their hands should try clamping them over their mouths"

I have seen this far too often, the hands wander, they begin to explore, they scratch, they fiddle, they turn into teenage spiders and can soon become the focus of the entire audience – not good.

Usually a presenter will put their hands in their pockets to bring them under control, but alas, the fiddling continues (you can imagine that this is possibly even worse). At best, the audience concentrate on how much change you have in your pocket as you jingle merrily away and try to decipher if you have enough money for a latte – once again not great and quite a distraction.

I have seen presenters fiddle with pens, microphones, wireless mice, buttons, belts, jewellery, imaginary pockets, with wedding rings (oh I wonder if he has just got married, I wonder if he is happy, he looks sad, I wonder what's going on there?... distraction, distraction, distraction). Let's bring these hands under control and give them something useful to do.

Build gestures into your presentation from the start. Consider where you can use your hands for counting, pointing out position, for indicating order, for imploring your audience, for measuring the temperature of an idea, for rolling the thinking forward, for emphasising that actions should stop or the results are enormous etc. etc. etc.

Imagine which gestures I am making as I think through these ideas:

- The deficit is large but the risk to the Euro is even larger
- To capture the market we will need to act fast
- There are tough times ahead but we can battle through

When you are at a party, down the pub, explaining how your journey was, talking about your day etc. you use gestures naturally and fluidly to emphasise and add visual character to the words you are using (our friends on the continent are even more emphatic when visually telling a story) so this is something you are used to. Take this natural ability and consider how best to adopt this in your presentation – build it in.

Keep these teenage spiders under control when you are between gestures too. The classic 'steeple' (hands together, finger tips touching, resting in front of the body at waist height) is ideal. Don't allow your hands to wander and let you down. Be in charge and keep them ready for action when required.

My daughter recently had to perform a speech in front of her class as part of her GCSE English course. We worked through the piece a number of times, focusing on delivery and overcoming her nerves, and to put icing onto the cake, we introduced a few simple hand gestures to add power to her performance. It worked well, she enjoyed the experience as did her class mates. It doesn't have to be much, but it has to be something. I am not suggesting you work so many actions into your show that it feels unnatural and rather staged, but be human, be yourself and let your emotion show through into your work.

When we are reading the body language of others, what their hands are doing is usually a massive giveaway.

The extremities (hands and feet) are the most difficult parts of our body to control – possibly due to the fact that they are quite far from the brain.

Observe what the hands are doing and step inside the heads of your audience (small groups or individuals) and discover what is **not** being said. It is almost like you have access to a secret diary so you can change the way you interact based on a complete picture, rather than just what is being said or how the words are being delivered.

Look for those gestures that indicate an emotional response (adaptors) such as the drumming of fingers which is usually a sign of impatience or frustration, or the tugging or straightening of hair which is a classic indication of unease or nervousness.

The touching of the face and neck can also be a great indicator of an uncomfortable situation, even to the point where the truth is being avoided.

The key here is to look for clusters of gestures and movements (and eye signals) which are not in keeping with an individual's usual behaviour – something tells you that things are not quite as they seem. Our instinct is usually an accurate gauge as to genuine behaviour or situations where something simply doesn't add up.

If someone uses non-typical gestures or giveaways that we suspect harbour ulterior motivations, then we can explore in more depth with a few well worded questions.

I would much rather have individuals and audience members on the same page as me, so I work hard to observe any indications that tell me where they are at, and work just as hard to bring them back online if they have taken an unexpected diversion.

Voice

Remember those rather un-nerving statistics - 38% of everything that an audience remembers from a presentation is based on the tone of voice used – your voice is, after all, the main vehicle for conveying your message, so let's make the most of our vocal performance.

Try to adopt a conversational tone and allow your personality to shine. Of course, if you don't have a personality, then this may be a little tricky.

Vary your tone, your pace and your volume. This verbal 'highlighting' will bring your presentation to life, and show your audience how interested you are in your own content – does it sound exciting to you? If you love it and it sounds like you do, then that enthusiasm will go a long way in pulling your audience into your world.

I like to lower the volume when I am approaching a very important part of my message. As I become quieter, the audience have to work that little bit harder to hear me and they have to concentrate that little bit more; you can almost see them leaning forward and turning their ear to the front to capture the information. You need to be careful that you are still audible when trying this, but give it a go and see how it brings your audience closer.

Speaking at a lower volume tends to slow down your delivery too, so if you are one of those presenters who find themselves rushing through their content, try a softer approach for a more controlled performance.

Imagine if you were delivering your presentation from behind a curtain or via an audio conference – how would that affect your vocal routine?

There is a great deal of information on the subject of voice and paralanguage (how we say things) and specialist coaches available to assist with projection, authority and a host of verbal tricks of the trade, but our *Feet on the Ground* approach begins with you being yourself and working with your strengths. Think about your words and how you can use your style to bring out the best in the way your message is delivered. Take your time, breath, and sip water to keep your mouth lubricated and ensure you are clear.

While on the subject of voice, let's not forget the incredible power of the **pause**. We should all be using regular pauses to add controlled drama to our performance. Whenever we make an important point, a pause will give the audience time to digest our words and the wisdom contained within. You can also use the pause to punctuate and to provide added emphasis as and when required. Pauses will also allow you to build anticipation and in doing so will enable you to enthral your audience. You are in charge, take your time and control the pace of your delivery to maximise your impression.

I like to pause before I begin any presentation. Make your way to your presentation 'zone' and before you begin look the audience in the eye and count to three (in your head ideally).

Longer pauses before you make an incredibly important point or directly after you have delivered a key message add power and authority to your words. (See Chapter 18 for an easy way to pause like an animal – your audiences will be wild for it).

Filler Alert!

A word about those annoying and almost invisible (to us) filler words.

Because we are human and like to think on our feet, we have a tendency to fill any empty void of silence with sounds. Usually these are fairly innocuous such as 'erm', 'err' and 'um' which can grate after a while; especially once you have spotted them. I once attended a poor series of presentations in which management (I won't name the company) were summarising the year gone by and the plans for the year ahead for their staff, and one of the presentations, which lasted only 20 minutes, contained 118 unnecessary uses of 'err', 'erm' and 'and', and this presentation was not the worse of the bunch! [I just want to take a moment and enjoy the fact that I have put the word 'and' three times in a row in that sentence and it makes grammatical sense – ok, moment over].

Some filler words are even more dangerous. I have heard the phrase 'the other thing I would like to say is...' used over and over in the same presentation which was followed by an overabundance of the words 'moving on'.I have also had the unfortunate experience of sitting through a 40 minute presentation in which the presenter used the words *'in respect to that'* before almost every point made – no idea why and, not surprisingly, quite a laughable distraction.

A business leader I know was asked in a formal press conference whether the levels of staff redundancies were likely to increase and his answer was:

"Er, er, er, er, er, er no."

This, as you can imagine, reduced somewhat the definite intention that he had planned with his answer.

Let's work to keep these 'fillers' under control – they are a massive diversion from the flow that you are looking to achieve and, once your audience hooks onto them, they will be more interested in counting how many times you say the same filler word than on the important messages you have for them.

If you have the chance to video your presentation or rehearse in front of friends, colleagues or family members, then hopefully any obvious filler foibles will be spotted so you can begin working to eradicate them from your performance.

Not only do we need to concentrate on the body language we are using to add emphasis to our words, therefore increasing the chance that our message will be taken on board in a convincing way, but we must not forget to take on board the two way street aspect of the body language conundrum.

As we know, we are always communicating in one way or another. Our ability to accurately read the body language of others and react accordingly, will massively increase our chances of making the right impression and having our information received and understood.

Watch carefully; consider what is going on in the minds of your audience, review their body language, look out for obvious signs of confusion, boredom, distraction, and impatience and react accordingly (and I don't mean by raising your voice and pointing).

If we notice our audience becoming agitated, for example shuffling feet, whispers and furrowed brows, we should address the cause/s of the unrest. Perhaps the room is too warm, or the audience are struggling to hear you, or a contentious point has been made and has not been backed up with enough substance. If we can read this response in our listeners, then we at least have an opportunity to do something about the cause and regain control of our show.

Too many presentations I have seen are simply boring (sadly) and at no point does the presenter do anything to decrease the onslaught of tedium. If you find your audience drifting and zoning out of your control, then change direction, change the pace, ask some questions, bring the involvement level back on track – don't ignore the signs that your audience are switching off.

Watch, accurately interpret, question and respond effectively – you are in charge of your presentation so let's make sure we address any potential derailment before it brings our show to an uncomfortable and unsuccessful conclusion.

The use of body language is a huge subject and we could spend unnecessary pages working on various techniques, gestures and poses which all deliver a particular feeling or point or stance on a subject, but if we look too deep we run the risk of losing the 'you' in your presentation.

Audiences want to hear from you, you are the expert, or at least you are the person that has the information the audience needs.

In the words of King Louie (from Jungle Book) – 'walk like you, talk like you...' (ooooo do be do). Too much emphasis on 'false' body language, the kind that makes you feel uncomfortable and makes your performance unnatural, will not aid your cause.

It is important to work in some body action and to control those teenage spiders, who will let you down if you turn your back on them. Effective and powerful body language will add huge value to your delivery. But, this has to sit well with you and who you are. Be human and allow yourself to relax into your style of presenting and apply some body language techniques, as explained here, into the mix to allow your story to permeate in the most effective way possible.

Summary Chapter 6 – *Taming the teenage spiders*

There is a great deal we can say on effective use of body language (there are complete books on the subject) but we need to focus on the aspects that will add value to our presentation and increase the power and passion of our performance.

Don't forget that over 90% of the impact you make will not have anything to do with the actual words you are using so add some space with appropriate body language action.

We are all communicating, all of the time so ensure you are under control of what your body is doing and look for clues from your audience that will tell you how well you are doing.

7. Treasures in the Undergrowth

Now we have explored the power of body language you can use this to enhance every interaction you will ever have, adding power and passion to the delivery and impact of all of your presentation opportunities. Solet's take a look at a few less obvious ways to really drive that message home.

Spanking the audience

Sounds a little radical doesn't it, and probably not a sub heading found in many presentation guides, but this proves the point well. I am not suggesting that you physically spank your audience (although some may enjoy this break from the norm – especially with the rise of popular novels such as *50 Shades of Grey*) but deliver your information in a brand spanking new way – spank your audience with a fresh and original take on the detail. Deliver your material in a way that is innovative, shake it up a little, provide a new take on the data and create renewed interest in your subject.

Try giving your facts and figures in a picture format – 'our annual production of bottle tops is equivalent to 77 Jumbo Jets!' is far more memorable than any tonnage figures, for example.

As we all know, modern business thrives on innovation, movement and change so we should be at pains to ensure our information is as new as it can be and is interpreted in the freshest way possible. Stay ahead of the curve and your audiences will be delighted to join you at the forefront of your market.

The power of **'fresh'** will give your communication the spark that immediately sets it apart from the type of presenters who struggle to make it off the launch pad.

Infect your audience

Some may suggest that audiences suffer from infection already as they look out upon a sea of zombies struggling to stay awake in a badly ventilated presentation arena, but I am talking about the type of infection that will boost your viewers and should not be feared.

Infect them with your enthusiasm, trust me, they will love you for it. Have you ever watched someone on stage that is simply bubbling with passion and zeal? It's almost impossible not to be drawn in and infected with this upbeat delivery.

One of the things I love about delivering the *Invisible PowerPoint* show, is the fact that the whole performance is designed to be fast paced and light hearted and audiences can't resist the tempo as they are pulled along by the tide of enthusiasm.

We should enjoy what we do, don't you agree? It makes us much better company and our audiences will respond to our fervour.

Smile and watch as your audience tune in to your pace and vitality, and then buckle up 'cause it's gonna be quite a ride.

Once they are on-board, you can guide them through the fabulous journey that will help make your information both fascinating and memorable.

Tease them to please them

A really effective way to entice your audience and ensure they are eager for your information is to...

.... tease them with it first. This is easier than it sounds. If you have an important or interesting piece of information (for your audience's sake I hope you do) then before delivering it, tell them how important it is or how interesting it is going to be. Once they know; draw this process out a little, build the anticipation, make them want it real bad and then pow, you can deliver the detail they are gagging for.

If you are really cruel you can even frustrate your audience a little further by not revealing this pearl of a snippet and make them wait until later in your presentation. A word of warning here though – if you are going to build it up and build it up and make it something all the audience begin to crave, then please make sure it is something all of the audience will want to hear.

Open the wound and scratch it

Another method of selling your story is to build a need for the information you are about to give – opening the wound – and highlight the benefits that this information will deliver and the resulting payback which will follow – scratching the wound. Sounds a little sadistic doesn't it, but it maintains that hunger for your information.

For example, if you were presenting details to your sales team about the new bonus scheme (seems feasible) you could begin by setting the scene around the benefits of having additional income.

"Wouldn't it be fabulous to bring home additional earnings, enough to pay off the credit card every month? Extra cash to spend on your loved ones and a little spare to treat yourself to those golf clubs you've been looking at?" "Naturally, as we are all in sales, we are used to being hungry for more and pushing ourselves to achieve. It is only right that this achievement is rewarded, we deserve it and it would be really handy to have access to additional funds for that holiday in the sun that we all deserve."

You have well and truly set the scene, **opened the wound**, and can now scratch at it as you go through the bonus scheme details, highlighting the benefits in a language that engages your audience and builds rapport throughout.

Psychology rocks

The amount that we enjoy something has a large bearing on how we are introduced to the idea, what we are led to believe about the experience, and this part of our presentation is very much in our hands. In fact, it is our duty to outline the benefits and value of our information if we truly wish to communicate to win.

When I introduce the *Invisible PowerPoint* show, I set the scene in a way that excites the audience, I build the anticipation and talk about *PowerPoint* (not something that usually excites an audience) in a way that engages and makes my audience say 'yes' to my show. I tell them how awesome it is going to be and promise to revolutionise their view of *PowerPoint*.

Not many presenters use the word 'awesome',which I think is a shame. I know it is a word that has generally been hijacked by a younger demographic and can be used (by them) to describe everything from a packet of crisps to a night of banging tunes (I recently heard it used often by the BBC to describe the Olympic Games in London), but when used to describe a presentation it certainly catches the ear.

And that is the idea – catch the ear, excite your audience and set the mood as one which will be not only fulfilling, but pretty dam useful too.

Imagine the two following menus:

Egg & Chips £ 4.50

Or…

Locally sourced, freshly laid barn eggs with organically grown Suffolk potatoes; hand cut, gently fried and seasoned   £ 4.50

They are both 'egg and chips' but I am looking forward to the second one much more than the first, and your audience will be too if you wrap your presentation up in a way that entices their interest and starts the brain's taste buds drooling.

This is the reason we should introduce our presentations in an upbeat and tantalizing way, and why those of us who are tempted to begin with an apology or excuse are really not doing ourselves any favours.

Summary Chapter 7 – Treasures in the undergrowth

There are a number of techniques we can use to increase the impact of our show.

Ensure your information looks and feels fresh – don't simply re-tell the same old information that audiences have heard a number of times before, give it to them in a new and innovative way.

Show them how enthusiastic you are about your subject, enthusiasm is infectious so spread this energy around the room.

Highlight the benefits throughout and don't be afraid to tell your audience how great your show is going to be and how valuable the information will be for them.

Audiences so rarely experience any of these techniques so do yourself, and them, a massive favour, and shake things up a little by adding some of this exceptional treasure.

8. **Nerves and Confidence Building**

Dry mouth, trembling knees, that feeling of nausea deep within your stomach, shaking hands, perspiration, the need to go to the toilet...again – sound familiar? Well, you are not alone if you have ever felt any of these symptoms of nerves.

Presenting is scary stuff – let's get that out of the way to start with. You are putting your ego on the line and allowing yourself to be judged by your audience. You are probably stepping out of your comfort zone and there is nowhere to hide.

Terrifying or exciting? Or both?

What's the worst that can happen? Actually, let's re-phrase that, what's the best that can happen? Let's begin moving away from our tendency to always look at the worst case scenario when considering our presentation opportunities. A great deal of fear is based on the assumption that things are going to go wrong, or our performance is not going to do us justice, or our audience is going to be judgemental, but this kind of thing hardly ever happens and our preparation is going to take care of any of these rare occurrences anyway.

I once read that **F.E.A.R** stood for False ExpectationsAboutReality which is a useful way to look at our fears. Nerves are perfectly natural and the adrenalin they create can be used rather than avoided.

Fear can be regarded as a software issue not a hardware problem. We are not born with all of this fear, but as we travel through life being told we can't do this or that,we begin to programme our minds leaning to the negative rather than the positive.

It seems strange but true that we tend to assume the worse rather than the best outcome from any random situation.

A few Halloweens ago, I took my son out for some 'trick or treat' action and, being of the age where it is far from cool to be seen with your dad, my son walked the streets with one of his friends.

Not a problem, they were never going to be far from the car as my duties as taxi driver around town were still required (clearly it is cool to have a set of wheels and a chauffeur) and I could keep an eye on them and make sure they didn't run into any bother.

As I watched from the comfort of my warm car (not a bad part of the deal really) they progressed to the bottom of the street and around the corner.

They were now out of sight.

Still out of sight...

Surely they will be round the corner shortly and back in view.

Hold on a minute, what if theyhave run into some older kids and have had some issues, or had a row with someone on their doorstep?

Still no sign.

How long before I walk down the street and see if they are ok?

Did I see some bigger kids down that end of the street?

Well, I waited and worried until they popped up in front of the car having taken a cut through to the next street (which I didn't know was there) and worked their way back towards where I was parked having a great time along the way.

Now, am I daft to worry about my son? No, of course not, but why did I assume that bad stuff had happened? Why did it not occur to me that good stuff was happening and all was well?

I am not alone – we all tend to imagine the negative instead of the positive and this is the same when we are asked to present. What if I mess it up, what if the technology fails, what if I freeze or make a fool of myself?

For some, this fear becomes a barrier and ensures we do everything in our power to avoid having to present, and in today's busy workspace, this will hold you back.

For others, this fear will simply prevent you performing at your best, so let's see if we can surmount this hurdle and overcome our *'software'* issue.

Try to re-programme your mind – plant flowers (the good stuff) not weeds (the bad) in your mind and let them flourish. Think of the positive outcomes rather than focusing on the negative. This will take a little practice but it is so, so worth it.

Next time you have a presentation opportunity, instantly think of the best outcome possible from your performance and consider other occasions when you performed well and had a similarly positive outcome. If we all decide to plant flowers in our minds what a colourful time we will have, and I guess it will smell good too.

We all have our strengths

A great way to overcome your fears about presenting and to increase your confidence while on stage (and beyond) is to spend as much time as you can working with the stuff you do best.

Sounds obvious I know. But if you have a really good voice, use it, if you have a magnetic personality, use it, if you are great at telling stories,work a number into your performance. If you are able to speak with feeling and sincerity, then let this flow through your time with your audience.

It makes sense to ask those close to you what you are really good at and what they like most about you, and allow this into your presentation. The audience want you, so the best bits of you are going to go down a storm.

The cloak of invisibility

Hiding your nerves is not as difficult as it sounds, and you do not need something borrowed from Harry Potter to achieve a confident looking performance.

You are in control, after all, so walk tall, allow fluidity into your movements and be enthusiastic from the start – audiences will really buy into your enthusiasm.

If you are one of these people who tends to shake with either excitement or nerves, try using small note cards (with your information on) rather than larger pieces of A4 paper which will advertise every tremble.

In the past, when I have been playing poker and have a particularly good hand, I used to find it difficult to hide the excitement that my excellent cards were causing within me – my hands tended to shake a little and it felt as though my whole body was giving the game away as my pulse quickened. These giveaways (tells) need to be brought under control (unless you're using them for bluffing purposes – aha tricky stuff...) so I worked on each of the signs and transformed my game. I now place my cards and hands on the table (this keeps them stable and ensures I don't move them) and I have adopted some discreet breathing techniques to slow my heart rate and keep my composure.

All I need now is to work on my card play, my mathematics, and my bluffing, and I will be ready for Vegas!

This is exactly the same for any of you who have nerve or fear issues – we need to apply some techniques to reduce this anxiety and build your confidence.

Another giveaway of the nervous presenter, is a lack of clarity in the voice. Have you ever suffered from 'dry mouth'? Take water with you when you present and sip regularly to keep your voice in a lubricated state. Take your time when sipping too, no need to rush, try not to catch half of your sip in your mouth and the other half on your shirt.

I find it useful to have my notes in the same place as my water. This enables me to combine a drink with a pause for thought and a little check of the notes to ensure I am on target and on message. This takes the pressure off, and allows you to maintain control of your presentation, and your audience won't mind in the slightest.

I can't cope! I can't do it!.....Yes you can

Here are a few strategies to enable you to deal with that sinking feeling and the overwhelming desire to run, run away.

Rehearse, rehearse, rehearse, is the simplest form of preparation and the best way to keep on top of those nerves.

Do you remember the first time you asked someone out on a date? Practicing in front of the mirror, the build-up, the aftershave/perfume, the butterflies and the euphoria once you had stepped out of your comfort zone and asked the question? Awesome stuff, and most definitely less scary the more times you ask.

Well the same is true of presenting (as with most things new) the first time is somewhat terrifying, and is something you are going to have to work through to make it to the less worrying second and third and fourth time.

If you rehearse a number of times, your content, your visuals and your story begin to sink in, and this will make a massive difference to both your performance and your state of mind on the day.

A word of warning, however,I am not talking about rehearsals in your head; those speedy run-throughs that are half directed by your ego and make everything seem easy and fool proof.

I am talking about physical, out loud, acted out, full run-through practice sessions, ideally in front of an audience, even a disinterested pet will do, but make it feel real.

Rehearse again.

And again (trust me, you will be grateful in the long run).

Now you are getting there and hopefully it will all be beginning to flow. This way you can iron out any issues with timing, and any confusion that may occur with your slides and explore the best way to deliver your information.

During my workshops, each of the delegates has to present – we keep this down to a 5 minute presentation to keep things fluid and light, and I ask each performer before they begin 'have you rehearsed?'

Without fail the best presentations are delivered by those who have taken the time to prepare properly, including an out loud full rehearsal. Those who rehearse in their heads only are the ones I have to stop after about 10 minutes of rambling (out loud presentations always take longer than in the head ones, so rehearse properly to check the timing if nothing else).

Those who have not rehearsed in any way, usually come across as the most nervous and their presentations are the poorer because of it.

It's not rocket science is it?

Another coping strategy is to have a checklist of everything you need for your show (don't leave anything to chance) and test all of your technology way in advance – you don't want to be flapping when you should be relaxing and applying some reassuring breathing techniques.

Talking of breathing, I suggest that you do, before, during and after your presentation – it makes for a much happier and longer existence. To keep the nerves to a minimum, try to take a big breath in through your nose while counting to 4, and then a big breath out (of your mouth) while counting to 8 – repeat this 4 times and allow yourself to relax. This will feed the vocal chords with more air and the brain with more oxygen, which has to be a good start.

A few home truths about your audience

Once you can work through your nerves, you are going to have a great time. The reason all will be well is because your audience are on your side. No one goes to a presentation hoping it will be poor and tedious; the audience want you to be entertaining, to educate them with style, and for your presentation to be a huge success.

You have the knowledge that your audience needs and wants to hear, you are the expert and they are hungry for what you know and what you have in store for them.

The audience certainly don't know you are nervous, so please, please don't tell them. If you adopt the strategies we have discussed in this chapter, there is no reason to suspect that they will witness your nerves or fear in the slightest, and a fabulous time will be had by all.

Summary Chapter 8 – Nerves and confidence building

Change your mind-set – don't think "what's the worst that can happen", reprogram your thinking to "what's the best that can happen".

Work to your strengths, make the most of your best assets and try to avoid the things that you struggle with.

Rehearse, rehearse and rehearse again – trust me, it's worth it.

The audience are generally on your side, they want your presentation to be a success.

If you are nervous, there is no need to tell the audience or to mention any aspects of your show that you are unhappy with. In my experience it is very unlikely that the audience will pick up on your nerves or notice any unsteady areas of your performance.

9. Visuals

So we have looked at the visual side of <u>us</u> and the body language expectations that we should place on ourselves to benefit our audience, so now let us make a few observations about the other visual aspects of our show.

Firstly, the stats tell us that visuals are good. The right visuals tend to increase the impact and memorability of our information. It is believed that the most effective visual aids can increase the retention of your spoken content by up to 70%. That is a stat that is worth working towards as 70% more of whatever your presentation goal is, sounds like a fantastic result.

We live in a TV age and our audiences like a few visual signposts during this journey of communication, so let's give them exactly that.

Our visuals must take our audience forward along the path of our presentation. Let's be careful not to provide distractions but enhance and add value to the mix.

During my *Invisible PowerPoint* show, I juggle with lemons to illustrate this essential point.

I'm a big fan of using props during presentations. Out come the lemons and up they go into the air as I talk about visual aids – this tends to freak the audience out a little, I am not sure how many presentations out there include juggling with lemons (not enough I say).

So the point I am making while the lemons spin up and down on a presentation journeyof their own, is that visual aids are exactly that, an 'aid' to your performance, designed to take your message forward. At this point I drop the lemons (on purpose, usually) and make the statement that we are talking about **visual aids** and not **visual distractions**.

At this stage, I explain the value of great visuals and the problem with pointless, misplaced, and distracting images – having distracted the audience with the juggling to drive this point home.

Sounds a little 'out there' but is definitely a powerful way to illustrate my point and is something all audiences remember.

Simply obvious

All of your visuals should fall into the category of 'simply obvious'; as soon as you have to go into detail, describing what your visual represents or apologise for the busy and complex image you are using, then you and your audience have missed the point.

There are exceptions to this rule, of course, for example, when you are looking to confuse or distract your audience for dramatic effect or to demonstrate a particular point – there are always exceptions to the rules and as long as you pitch it right, then why not go for the 'unusually effective' approach.

Imagine a presentation exploring the new company structure which has simplified departments, reporting, systems, and represents a scaled down and streamlined approach to business. This style of presentation could handle a complex and confusing visual (the company before the re-structure) as long as this is balanced with a secondary slide which represents the new, rationalised

78

organisation. A before and after style of delivery – I like the sound of that.

On the whole, however, your visuals should not need explanation; the important point should stand out and be immediately obvious. Generally the big, bold, and brilliant visual will stand you in good stead and make your message more powerful and memorable.

As soon as you have to explain the meaning of a particular image, then you are burdening your audience with additional work and they tend to switch off if this is the case.

Think of the images and graphics you see during the news to illustrate a story. These visuals are usually powerful and obvious and on the whole need little clarification.

A look of confusion across the room is rarely a good sign, so ensure your visuals flow from the screen and your message is clear and organised; use arrows if needs be, cut down on detail and don't be afraid of employing plenty of space.

Think signposts, not wallpaper.

The **less is more** philosophy is no truer than here in the use of well-constructed and effectively targeted visual aids. Maintain the focus and allow your visuals to be the musical accompaniment that adds flavour to your presentation.

Adding power to your points

It would be remiss of me not to mention *PowerPoint* in our chapter all about visuals, so let's explore the why and how of effective *PowerPoint* slide shows.

It seems strange that everybody's doing it and very few of us like it – a bit like paying taxes, I suppose. Clearly something about the whole *PowerPoint* process is outdated. So let's find out...

Let's not beat around the bush, and this may shock you, but dozens and dozens of slides, packed with multiple bullets and more text than a teenager's mobile, does not make for an awe inspiring presentation experience.

There, I've said it – it's here, in print, that kind of presentation does not work. We've all sat through them and we've all created them and now is the time to **stop it**. No more.

If you can recount a healthy fraction of any of the information communicated in a deck of complex, bullet heavy, and 'read to the audience' slides, then you are the exception to this rule. But even you must change the way you construct and deliver your presentations, for the sake of the rest of us who can't take it all in, and need an exceptionally strong coffee to confirm we are still alive.

However, that said, *PowerPoint* is still a very useful tool. It is a great way to enable the visual markers that we, in our TV age, find so engaging.

A useful guide when using *PowerPoint* is to ask yourself the question:

"Can the slide do a better job than ME? And if so, how can it?"

Our visuals are only one half of our double act. *PowerPoint* is the half where our graphs, our charts and diagrams live. These slides can act to illustrate your story, but should not be relied upon to tell it. The human side of the presentation is where **you** come in, and you are better than *PowerPoint* at anything which requires emotion, passion, enthusiasm, and most importantly, anything wordy.

Text on slides is the number one turn off that I see used and abused again and again. When people talk about 'death by *PowerPoint*' (and they do, all the time) they are referring to wordy slides, multiple bullets and text, text, text.

Some words on a slide work, for example regular headings are a useful way to keep our audiences on track, and some important messages need to be written word for word and displayed, but generally text on slides is not great.

There is only so much text based information we can take on board – it's a bit like asking a stranger for directions, you tend to switch off after the first few turnings and an occasional roundabout.

Like a fine sauce, reduce, reduce, reduce the words on your slides and enhance the flavour by using your own, individual, secret recipe input. If you can give them the real you, your audiences will love it, rely on the slides to tell the story, and your audience will despise youfor eternity!

PowerPoint is fabulous for sucking up your time and eating away at your day. Slide after slide of information – all the good stuff that we know about a topic, and quite often all of the rotten stuff we know too, all appear on multiple slides with groovy transitions and pretty fonts and colour schemes. STOP IT, please. Simple is good.

Simple and consistent slide style benefits your audience and your schedule. Complexity and slides that resemble a pair of clown's trousers are not considered too highly in any corporate meeting environment.

Two fonts and two colours are more than enough, and those transitions that you can find that do whizzy things to your page turns and text reveals, if they do not add specific value (I've not seen any that do) then do not include them.

Focus good, distractions bad.

Don't forget that your story and your objectives are by far the most important part of any *PowerPoint* – don't allow the technology to get in the way of this. Ensure your audience congratulate you on an awesome presentation, not a fabulous slide show.

Summary Chapter 9 – Visuals

The <u>right</u> visuals are incredibly useful for your audience and can aid your performance, increasing your impact considerably.

Think of the visuals you choose as signposts, not wallpaper, they must add value and guide your audience through your content effectively.

Ensure your visual is the best method of putting your particular point across. Can the slide do a better job than you to communicate a particular point? Sometimes they can, but sometimes they fall woefully short so use sparingly but use well.

10. **Humour**

There is a great deal we can learn from the stand-up comedian, but we need to tread very carefully if we are tempted to use humour as part of our knockout presentation.

Three guys walk into a pub; an Englishman, an Irishman and a Scotsman, they bump into an Essex girl and my oh my they enter a storm of political correctness that becomes the focus of their presentation and the main content of the show is forgotten.

The professional comedians can get away with most things, but we can't – it's as simple as that.

If you get it right, then humour is a fabulous way to build rapport and relax an audience, and makes for extremely powerful communication. Get it wrong and it will kill your presentation stone dead.

Audiences like it if you can laugh at yourself, it comes across as being human and approachable, but you need to tread very carefully. Think of those presentations where you have sat in the audience and the presenter has 'tried' to be funny – it is embarrassing for all concerned, but measure this against a light hearted presentation that has the right sprinkling of effective humour, and you have something that is enjoyable and memorable – a very rare presentation indeed.

I like it, though, so I tend to give my presentations a fun feel (where I know it will be well received – some audiences won't go for it). I will put my audiences at ease and allow them to relax into my style.

This way,I have full control over the tempo and the drama of the show and am able change the pace when I need to crank things up for the serious stuff.

This is when presentations become communication that wins. You are in control, you know your stuff, and you have prepared like a professional – the stage is yours – why wouldn't it be amazing?

There are a number of techniques you can use to give your show an amusing feel that are much safer than any mother-in-law jokes, so let's have a look at a few options.

Here's one for you...

Audiences love a story or two (or three or four) in a presentation.Use the power of the personal anecdote to engage and entertain. These real life experiences (yours or someone else's) about life, love, the office, the traffic, the children, pets, holidays, hobbies etc. are ideal.We are all used to telling them at home, at work, and at play, which means our delivery will be natural and fuelled with the confidence of familiarity.

Use these stories to make a point during a presentation – here's an important point and here's a story to reinforce this point. Not rocket science but so, so effective.

(More about stories coming up real soon...)

It's like...

Working with analogies can give your ideas real zing. Comparing two objects or ideas can easily be re-worded to deliver a comic impact. If you start looking out for these, you will find numerous examples that you can then change to suit your topic or ideas.

"Our sales strategy looks like it has been written by the same team that write flat pack furniture instructions"

"This approach is like looking for fish by climbing a tree!"

Anything along these lines can be adapted to add power to your performance.

I say I say I say...

Humorous quotations are such a simple way to liven up your content and your audience. Easy to find and deliver, and resonate with most audiences.

When we hear the words from a famous source, we tend to pay more attention and our information is given additionalprestige.

Try surprising your audience by using quotations from some unlikely sources such as Homer Simpson, Edmund Blackadder, Clint Eastwood or any other source that raises an eyebrow:

"You can't stay in your corner of the forest waiting for others to come to you. You have to go to them sometimes."

Winnie the Pooh

Easy huh?

Ooh look at that...

Funny signs and cartoons are also a breeze to find online, and once tied to a point you want to make, are an ideal source of both unexpected and potent graphic reinforcement.

Nothing adds more relief to a corporate *PowerPoint* than a little well placed humour, so give these ideas a try and breathe new life into your display.

Summary Chapter 10 – Humour

<u>Appropriate</u> humour can be really effective, but misplaced humour is a show killer.

Funny stories and anecdotes that allow you to laugh at yourself, if well placed, can add to the 'human' aspect of your performance and audiences generally warm to these.

I'm all for mixing it up and delivering information in a fresh and exciting way, but when it comes to humour, erring on the side of caution is sage advice.

Don't be afraid of it but think of your whole audience; if your humour is likely to offend even a single participant then you need to think again.

11. **Your Story**

We all have a story to tell, we may not think so if surprised with the probing question "so what's your story then?" but believe me we all have a story.

Think for a moment of all of those things that you have experienced over the last week which you have recounted to a colleague or friend – those things that either taught you a valuable lesson or reminded you of an important universal truth.

Go on, take a moment and think, what has been going on over the last few days?...

If you ponder reasonably hard the flood gates will open and the gems will begin to pour through. This is the beginning of your story.

These 'gems' may not appear to sparkle at first and may need a little polish before they are worthy to be put into your 'story' treasure chest, but they are there and you must make them work for you.

I recently attended a presentation by Manley Hopkinson (the adventurer and transformational leadership guru) which was delivered entirely as part of a story about a round the world yacht race. Within the story were messages about leadership, relationships and passion, which enthralled the entire audience.

It was a great story, superbly told and Manley is an incredibly likeable presenter, so a memorable event for all concerned.

We may not have adventures to the same extent as Manley, but we have experiences that allow us to deliver our message with power and conviction, and enhance our presentation and its impact for our entire audience.

Audiences love stories, and throughout history they have been used to transform ideas into reality.

More often than not, the stories are the part of the presentation that your listeners will remember, rather than your intricate graphs, charts, and bulleted lists of information.

Storytelling is a wonderful tool to put your point across in an alternative way that your audience will find easy to digest.

Make sure your stories have a point, however, as a meaningless story is a distraction you can do without during your show. Your meaning may not be immediately obvious, and a connection between your story and the message intended may take time to instil itself into the consciousness of your audience, but there must be a reason for using that particular story, and its purpose needs to be clear before the end of your show.

I know some presenters that tell stories in parts, stringing the eager audience along and ensuring they are paying attention throughout, and delivering the pay-off at the end of their presentation. If done well, this can be extremely effective, but it takes practise and requires the right kind of story.

Your story is the most important aspect of this process, as the personal anecdotes you can relate to your listeners will be the ones that strike a chord (more than any other 'this happened to someone else' type of story).

Personal stories bring presentations alive so much more than simple facts can. They give the message a context and build rapport incredibly quickly.

Try making a note of any experiences that provide you with a valuable lesson, or any stories that you hear that you feel could add value to the messages you are conveying to your audience.

If I think back over the last week, I have a trip to the cinema, a visit from my mother, an uncomfortable situation in my local pub, my daughter's first solo drive around the M25, a night out dancing, a blood donation, and a little bit of karaoke to choose stories from – without a doubt there will be material there to illustrate a point in any presentation I am in the process of creating. As long as it serves yours and your audience's purpose, you are on to something.

These stories will allow you to build valuable empathy and assist your communication no end.

I usually tell a lot of stories based around me and my kids as these tend to be universal (such as the one about my son Halloweening in chapter 8, or my daughter and her GCSE preparation in chapter 6); even those without children or who have yet to experience the roller-coaster that raising kids can be, at least know someone who has been though this 'wonderful' experience.

So add the real YOU into your communication, share your magic and tell the stories that can be related to the topic at hand.

Summary Chapter 11 – Your story

Audiences love stories. Anecdotes that are interesting, humorous, inspiring and engagingenable your listeners to understand your point in a more digestible.

When compiling your content think of the stories you can use to help your audience appreciate your meaning. It is these parts of your presentation that will be most easily remembered so tie them effectively to your main points and your content will be absorbed far more effectively.

Every presentation should contain stories – if yours doesn't then you must do something about this now. Your audiences will thank you for it.

12. Question Time

Hold on a minute, what's the *question time* chapter doing here, why is it not at the end of the book?

How many of you finish your presentations with question time? I would imagine 95% of all of the presentations I have seen leave the Q & A session right until the end. This is understandable, as this is the point where all of the information in the presentation has been imparted and it is here that an opportunity for the audience to ask a few questions fits well.

But, the end of your presentation is far too important to let it fizzle out with a possible lack lustre question and answer session. There are a number of things that we must try to achieve when closing our show, and the good old Q & A doesn't quite cut it.

I have seen a presentation experience ruined with a 'damp squib' question session at the end on more than one occasion, and it is such a shame and such a waste.

I was recently at a presentation for one of our country's top broadcasters and the content and delivery were ok. The host of the presentation, however, built up the part of the audience by suggesting that they were a lively and inquisitive crowd and would (no doubt) have plenty of questions at the end.

Well, no surprises for guessing what happened. The end came (and believe me the presentation was ok) and the host asked if anyone had any questions (to the audience of approximately 80 guests). Silence, silence and more silence. *"Any questions, anyone? Come*

on, surely there are some questions?" Go on pile on that pressure –
we will talk about how to encourage questions in a moment. *"Are
you sure there are no questions? Anybody?"* Still silence loomed
and now it's getting embarrassing for everyone – uncomfortable
doesn't do it justice. *"Anyone? Ok, you are **free** to go."*

Aaaarrrrghh! What a way to end a reasonable performance. What
a shame and what a waste of a great opportunity.

Now don't get me wrong, I am a fan of the Q & A session and most
presentations should have one. Presentations are an opportunity
to have a conversation with your audience and this needs to be a
two way experience to be most effective. However, the end of
your performance is not the best time for this to occur.

I like to have my question time **near** the end of the show, with
enough time to, firstly, allow for plenty of questions and secondly,
to explore any issue/s in more detail if there tends to be some
misunderstanding or a need to dig deeper into the subject.

But, and this is the key, I need time at the end of the show to
effectively close my presentation once the Q & A is taken care of –
very important this, and more about it later.

So Q & A good; fizzle, fizzle, drip, drip, not good. Let's explore how
to have a really useful question time, every time, and how best to
deal with the tricky, icky and sticky questions that may arise.

First and foremost, be encouraging – if you put your audience at
ease and allow their confidence in your subject to rise, then you are
far more likely to have a lively Q & A.

You can usually tell by the audience responses and body language
as you work through your material if they are likely to be engaging

you in inquiry, interrogation or icy silence. Be human and spend some time to watch their reaction as you endow them with your inspiring messages and be ready to deal with what you see.

I will often check with my audience at regular intervals that they are on track, understanding and appreciating the information. This way we begin to have a two-way dialogue and by the time we get to the formal Q & A, we are all ready for the flow to continue.

Some audiences will need more structured encouragement when it comes to asking questions. I like to ask the first question if the atmosphere is telling me a kick start is required. Something like "at this point of my presentation audiences are often thinking..." or "one of the questions that I regularly get asked is..." Once I have started the ball rolling, then it is far more likely that the audience's confidence begins to roll too, and we have therefore broken the ice on the water butt of question time and the rest of the questions can flow.

For larger groups who are a little reticent at getting stuck into the Q & A session, I tend to give them a moment to consider potential questions with the person sitting next to them (60 seconds is usually enough time for them to discuss potential questions and stay on message so they don't drift off into anything too chatty). It is far more likely that the confidence of two people combined will be enough to encourage some hands to be raised and the Q & A to begin.

Once a question has been asked,it makes sense to ensure your entire audience remain involved and engaged with everything that goes on.

Make sure you repeat the question back to the asker to ensure that everyone in the audience has heard the question – it's so disappointing when you are in an audience and the presenter begins to answer a question that, due to the size of the venue, the acoustics, or the lack of adequate audio support, you have not heard. Instantly you are side-lined and out of the game – a dangerous place for any audience.

Another reason to repeat the question is to make sure you have heard it correctly and understand the context within which it has been asked.

When you are ready to provide your answer give 20% of your attention to the person who asked the question (because we are all polite and lovely presenters) and 80% to the rest of the audience to keep them in touch with the developing subject. This way you retain control and encourage other questions to follow.

Attack Attack!

Generally, questions are asked by the interested, the confused and the inquisitive, but occasionally you will be confronted by a saboteur who is looking to steal the limelight or put you on the spot.

In my early days of presenting, when I worked for a sales and finance company, I thought it would be a good idea to present the idea of providing lease options to a manufacturer's sales team. Makes sense – a client wants to buy the product but doesn't have the capital available – bring in the finance team and a lease agreement and they can pay for the goods they need over an agreed period without the capital expenditure exposure.

This 'good idea' would add another string to the sales team's bow, making the sales process more flexible for their clients and provide value for our finance team too – win, win. The date was set and I took with me our finance expert, a very approachable and knowledgeable girl who knew her stuff and had all the charms required to win over any young sales team.

It wasn't until we pulled up in the car park that my able presentation assistant became my, not so able, presentation jelly.

Oh dear – finance was her bag, I was the sales guy with a bright idea, but without her I was in way over my head.

How bad can it be? A sales team of approximately 12 people who were on a similar wavelength to me – a reasonable sales tool to make their lives easier, and a brief presentation to introduce the idea...

My 'jelly' buddy, after many deep breaths and calming thoughts, plucked up the courage to sit at the back of the meeting and, if required, if I was struggling, would provide some assistance – as long as I didn't draw attention to her in any way. Hmmmmm.

You know that moment when Butch Cassidy and the Sundance Kid made a run for it at the end of the film only to find half the Mexican army waiting for them – well this was to be my 'cowboy' moment.

In we walked, and there they were – the entire company, sales, marketing, finance, management, everyone. To add a little more spice to the mix we were audio conferencing with the French office too – oh bugger!

Well I gave it a good go and did my best and almost pulled it off, that was until the Q & A. My 'jelly' buddy had almost dissolved into her seat and was avoiding all eye contact, and then the Head of Finance began asking his questions...

I later learned that he used to be a bit of a noise in the City and knew his stuff in all things finance and leasing. This, however, was not the problem. He didn't ask the sort of questions you would imagine, such as the interest rate we would apply across the term of the lease, the competitiveness of our package, or how we would make the process seamless for them, but all sorts of technical questions, deep rooted in the theory of finance – questions to make him look good and steal the limelight, and questions that I really shouldn't have even tried to answer. I was young and inexperienced and took his questions at face value but I was drowning. I looked to my 'buddy' and I think I heard her actually whimper – not a positive sound in the circumstances.

Experience now tells me that the Head of Finance was what we call in the industry a 'complete tosser' and his attempt at sabotage should have been tackled in a professional and effective way.

Here are some tactics you can use to avoid those instances when the questions are a little uncomfortable.

The 5 R's

Redirection   Sometimes we simply won't know the answer to a question – we are human after all (so many presenters aren't human by the way, they are robots – don't tell anyone though). It makes sense to own up if this is the case (to not knowing the answer, not to being a robot) and ideally, suggest that you can find out what the answer is for future use, but only if you really intend to find out what the answer is.

However, in this situation you can easily **redirect** the question to your audience, use the phrase 'does anyone have experience with this situation...?' or 'does anyone have any thoughts on this subject...?' or something similar to open the debate within your audience. Control the debate effectively and chances are your 'difficult' question will be answered and your audience will feel empowered and engaged into the bargain.

Reversing   When a question is asked with the specific intention of putting you on the spot, this uncomfortable situation can be **reversed** by asking the question directly back to the questioner. This way you can use their heavy handed approach and kick back to regain the initiative. Make sure you will not be walking into the classic 'I don't know, that's why I asked' scenario but use a soft and enquiring tone when asking the question back, act as if you are interested in their opinion and then you can move on or use another of these techniques to reduce the heat.

Rephrasing   Sometimes we will come under attack while we are presenting, never a comfortable experience but often our message may not be one that our audiences are thrilled to hear.

I recently attended a series of *'you are being made redundant'* presentations, which always have to be handled in a delicate way and, not surprisingly, there were some interesting and heated questions raised.

If you really don't want to answer a question you can try to **rephrase** it. Don't be tempted to ask the question back to the person who has asked it in this scenario but **rephrase** the question to your advantage, re-word it, carefully, and then you can proceed to answer it. This is a little underhand and you should be careful as to how much of a deviance you take when you re-craft the question, but it should allow you to maintain control of the presentation.

This technique is the politician's best friend. Listen to how they answer questions based on what they want to discuss even if these are not the questions originally asked. Politicians are a tad too blunt when they employ this skill – we can be far more persuasive.

It will take practice though so give it a go – how would you rephrase this question to take some of the heat out of the situation?

"Does this mean we have to re-write all of our traditional PowerPoint slide shows?"

Classic – and easily dealt with. Try some variations and see what you feel comfortable with – here are two rephrased options I would go with:

"So in effect you are asking if you need to abandon your traditional ways of working in this fast paced and ever moving market?" (Rephrased)

or

"I hear there are concerns that your existing experience will not be of use with the new methods of presenting, well, let me tell you this..."(Rephrased)

Or something that is relevant to your product or service.

You get the idea; sometimes this will keep things flowing rather than put you in an uncomfortable spot.

Revealing   Some questions are simply asked to open up a contentious issue or asked by someone spoiling for trouble (I think back to my finance saboteur once more). The trick in this case is to spot where the hidden agenda is coming from and expose it in a diplomatic way. I would advise against answering this kind of question without pausing to acknowledge your suspicions with phrases such as 'do you have some thoughts on that' or 'you seem to know something about this' – expose the feelings of the questioner in a polite way and have them talk first, then you can decide if an answer is appropriate for your audience or if you would rather answer this one to one after the presentation.

Once again, this tactic is to ensure you maintain control rather than letting your show be hijacked by someone with a cross to bear.

Repositioning   Another favourite of the politician, this bridge building technique allows you to move from a question that you would rather not answer to a topic you are happier to address.

Try to be convincing as though you are still answering the question rather than evading it but take the subject to a different place where you feel far more comfortable.

Phrases such as 'the real issue here is...' or 'what we really should be asking is...' or 'essentially, your question is about...' can be effective here so we can go from harsh questions about **price** to answering questions about **value**, or from questions about **redundancy** to questions about **long term profitability**. Don't be tempted to bridge too far but make life easier for yourself. Devise your own **repositioning** phrase and give it a go – practice on your kids first, if they buy it then you are home and dry.

All of these techniques can come in handy if you are up against it and would rather not be backed into a corner. They are an **occasional** substitute for the full, honest and informed answers we are regularly giving our audience and could help you along on your presentation journey.

If you are presenting material that your audience may find hard to hear, be aware throughout your show and keep on top of the feelings as you present. Check the temperature from time to time by being human and asking questions and deal with any preconceptions along the way:

"I appreciate that some of this information is not the brightest news you could hear but do you understand why we need to make these changes?"

Allow your audience to share their thoughts and emotions during your presentation so you can respond to issues before they arise and begin to fester.

The last thing you need is to battle on regardless and have an uncontrollable rabble building, unnoticed, within your audience.

You need to avoid lots of unanswered questions and frustrations being taken away from your show, as you will no longer be in a position to provide solutions and responses for your audience.

Be human, consider your audience, put yourself in their shoes and explore the questions and responses you would raise if you were sitting on their side of the stage. This way you will be suitably equipped for a healthy Q & A and any concerns you have will be minor ones. And if you are ever faced with the 'finance saboteur' you will be armed, ready to defend yourself and repel his tossiness.

Summary Chapter 12 – Question time

A healthy Q & A is a great asset to a presentation, but avoid having yours right at the end of the show.

Your **close** is far too important to let the Q & A get in the way.

Encourage questions and ensure your show is a two way conversation; it's healthy and allows you to address your audience on their level.

Don't be drawn in by any 'saboteurs', use some *creative* techniques to maintain control and avoid a situation that will make both you and your audience uncomfortable.

13. **Tales of Terror**

Have you ever been to a presentation and something unexpected has occurred? The projector has malfunctioned, your laptop is playing up, the link to your video file is based on material sitting on your home pc, your memory stick is looking for more up to date software, your video conference will not connect, the audience is three times the size you expected, your time slot has shrunk to a tenth of what you had prepared for...

Or, if you are really unlucky, a combination of all of these issues!

These things happen and they happen regularly, and as technology improves our lives and gives us a host of fantastic ways to communicate our message, the problem is only going to get worse.

Imagine you have turned up to present for an audience of 100 people and they are waiting expectantly, literally on the edge of their seats, poised to drink from your fountain of knowledge. You are prepared, you have some magic *PowerPoint* for them, you are ready to inspire, to entertain and to wow them in more ways than they thought possible... and then the projector goes pop...

Just as you were plugging your laptop in, it just died;"I didn't touch it, honest". Nothing to do with you, but sometimes the technology will fail us. Do you have a spare projector? No, neither does the venue, hmmmm – what is your next move?

Your audience, sadly, are not likely to be sympathetic and will expect your presentation – if the technology has failed you they will still expect your presentation and if you have nothing in reserve they will blame you. Crazy, I know, it's not your fault and you could kick yourself for not putting your projector into the car just in case, but your audience will still expect your presentation.

I suggest you give them exactly that – present to them, give them a taste of the real you, wow them with your knowledge, entertain them with your stories and enrich them with your experience.

The only problem is, if everything you have is connected to your slideshow then this is going to be one hell of a task.

The best presentations are sometimes the ones that take a huge deviation from what the audience expects. Our presentation which kicked off this book and inspired me to put word to page would have been so, so much better if our expert had just shared his knowledge, his story, his experiences of his market, and told us some anecdotes to illustrate this fountain of knowledge – instead we had a jumbled mess of half working technology and simply no magic.

If your technology fails, you must have a fall-back position, you must be ready with your 'show', it's just going to be a bit different from the one you originally planned, that's all.

I fear for those who rely 100% on their *PowerPoint*, or even worse, rely on someone else's *PowerPoint*.

What if your 50 slide presentation, which takes an hour to deliver, is all ready to go and due to the previous speaker, you only have a 30 minute time slot? Do you rush through your content, skipping through slides and glossing over your material and as the 30 minutes ticks away, increase your speed and whizz through the last ten slides? I hope not.

Once again, conditions you can't really control and that occur all the time and that require a plan 'B'.

What if you are ready to go on stage with your upbeat vision of the future, including expansion, development, diversification and a road map of future success, only to hear the previous presentation from the finance director highlighting cutbacks, redundancy and potential closures?

Let's hope this never happens as this one is highly avoidable, but what is your move?

I like to be human when I present, I consider my audience before, during, and after my show. What do they want and need from me as I prepare, as I deliver, and when I am no longer there?

Your audience do not need a rushed, jumbled, and stuttered attempt at a presentation, they need your well prepared, measured, and inspiring 'plan B'.

If you are sensible, you will have a cut down version of your slideshow for those times when the previous speaker has rudely trampled all over your time slot. If you are smart, you will have a fall back presentation that does not rely on your slides at all. And if you are a professional, you will have the wherewithal to recognise when your presentation is simply not appropriate and have an alternative approach to your material.

The easiest way to avoid the 'terror tales' is to know your stuff, inside and outside, back to front, and from every angle. If you have the knowledge that your audience crave then a healthy Q & A session instead of a slideshow can get you out of all sorts of trouble.

Be ready with a series of questions to kick off the session. Just as you would if your presentation was running as planned,**hook** your audience and **establish rapport** with your opening questions.

In a way, the pressure is off – the audience will be appreciative that you are able to 'carry on regardless' in the face of adversity and will hopefully be on your side (unless the problems are actually your fault, of course).

You will need to be creative, think on your feet and be ready with your stories and anecdotes to ensure the Q & A remains lively and entertaining, but this is where the real you can shine and your audience will respond accordingly.

Preparation is the key in all of the scenarios where there is a spanner in the works and you have to change direction. Those presenters who do not prepare for these kind of eventualities are missing a serious trick, as the preparation alone will make for a more rounded, considered, and entertaining presentation.

Chances are, we can all add another few 'terror tales' to this list, which goes to prove that this kind of thing happens with worrying regularity.

It doesn't have to be a worry for us though – we can cope, in fact, we can do more than cope, we can shine. But for things to shine they need a bit of a polishing first, so buff up, prepare, and think through your options and wow your audience whatever the circumstances.

Summary Chapter 13 – Tales of terror

Even in this highly technical age things will go wrong.

For reasons beyond our control the well planned and finely tuned presentation we have created will have to change with very little notice.

Know what your Plan B looks like, have it ready, be flexible and be prepared for alterations.

Can you deliver your show without slides? Can you give a well-rounded and unrushed summary of your information if your timeslot is cut in half? If not then you need to prepare and be ready.

The true professional can step up and deliver their magic whatever the circumstances – if all you have is Plan A then you may run the risk of letting yourself and your audience down.

14. **Closure**

Just like all the best stories, your presentation must have a start, middle, and an end, and psychologically your audiences need to feel your show nearing completion. If you have structured your message well, your listeners will not only see the end coming, but they will be ready for it too (in a good way, of course).

There are a few, very good reasons why I am not tempted to finish my presentations with a hearty Q & A, and most of these reasons live in the land of **closure**.

The end of your show is as important (if not more so) than your opening. The typical attitude to presenting of *"tell 'em what you're gonna tell 'em, tell 'em, and then tell 'em what you've told 'em"* continues to grate on me — no wonder we have to sit through countless, non inspiring, waste of everybody's time presentations.

I am all for a solid conclusion and a suitable summary, but let's approach these as the professionals we are, and make sure we don't miss a gilt edged opportunity.

Your presentation close should contain the following:

A **summary**, a powerful, thought provoking conclusion, our **wow moment,** and a specific and detailed **what's next**.

Summary

How tedious would it be if I simply recounted my information in a cut down format to sum up my show? We should know the answer to this because we have all sat through many a dreary summing up session.

How about we mix it up a little and summarise in an alternative way? You could use a story to review the content of your show, or perhaps a metaphor – I like to use a 'journey' metaphor to recap the highlights of what we have covered, and the key learnings we have uncovered.

Think of something that will be memorable and fitting for your audience. What about a topical news story that could mirror your show, or perhaps a well-known sporting event or a film outline? All sounds a little out there, I know, but this stuff really makes a difference.

If you want your content to hit home, give it a twist – like modelling a balloon animal, your professional twists will enable magic to happen.

Give it some thought – there is something not too far from home that will give your summary extra power and impact, and will breath new life into an area of the presentation that is usually an afterthought.

Wow moment

A big finish is a must for the end of your performance, just as it is at the end of any stage spectacular.

This is the moment that your audience will have fixed in their minds as you leave the stage and they leave the building, so, let's make it memorable.

If you allow your presentation to fizzle out with a lack lustre summary and a weak 'any questions' request, you are missingsuch an important trick, and just like missing your last bus home, this will make for a frustrating end to yours and your audience's day.

Give your audience something to remember, something that really sticks before you turn them loose once more into the world.

Don't be afraid to think big and innovate – you can be as creative as you wish here to drive your message home.

Stunning quotations, an amazing statistic, the best story from your treasure trove of experience,even an inspiring graphic can give your audience something to focus on rather than them desperately thinking where their next cup of coffee is coming from.

Wow them, blow their socks off, and enjoy the moment as your words are absorbed and your message connects both in body and in mind.

What's next?

At the close of my *Invisible PowerPoint* show, I like to stir the emotions a little and encourage my audience to think for themselves, while providing some useful guidance to suggest the path that would be most beneficial and amazing for them to take.

I usually close my show by encouraging everyone to take three simple steps –

1. The first is to step away from the 95% of all presentations that do not deliver on their promises, and prove to be an incredible waste of everybody's time.

2. The second is to step towards the 5% of those presenters who can inspire with focused delivery and influential messages, and are a joy to behold.
3. And thirdly, I ask them to step outside of their comfort zones, and allow themselves to be phenomenal.

With your '**what's next**' message, you must be clear and concise, so your instructions can be very specific.

Your audience can be told exactly what they will be doing differently, and what they will be doing next because of the information they have now received.

Quite often, we know what course of action we should take and we simply need someone else to give us the opportunity to empower this action. Sounds a little daft doesn't it? But how many times have you heard of a long term smoker (who would love to quit) but has beenrepeatedly unsuccessful until their doctor tells them that they <u>must</u> stop. This is the incentive they seem tohave been waiting for, and are then able to cease immediately.

Don't be afraid to be specific and demanding with your '**what's next**' request; your audience will not mind (unless, of course, your 'what's next' is to part with large sums of cash).

It is your duty as presenter to ensure that you deliver value for your audience. Don't miss this golden opportunity to deliver your conclusions with impact and style and make sure everyone who has had the good fortune to be listening takes away some powerful memories and a clear set of objectives for the journey ahead.

Summary Chapter 14 – Closure

The end of your show is the most important part of your time on stage and this needs to be highly crafted and rehearsed.

Be clear about your objectives and your goals and give yourself (and your audience) the best chance of success.

Summarise in a way that is highly memorable, be specific with your instructions and send your audience away ready to take the actions you prescribe.

Communicating to win is all about results – it is your responsibility to make success a reality.

15. **What Not to Do…**

I am all for experimentation, innovation, and trying something a little different, but in my experience there are a host of things that simply turn an audience off.

The worst examples

PowerPoint struggles here. I am sure we have all seen slides that are barriers to communication; rather than adding value to the information sharing process; they induce a tiredness usually reserved for the elderly and the Japanese executive.

A 90 page, bullet heavy *PowerPoint* immediately after lunch on a summer's afternoon, is usually a recipe for snoozville.

No one attends a presentation hoping it will be a feeding ground of tedium. We want new, fresh, informative and impressively interesting information.

The typical *PowerPoint* slide, with its royal blue background, green title (in capitals) with a shadow effect, followed by a weighty 9 bullet points, all introduced with an infuriating ticking transition sound effect, balanced by an uninspiring clip art image of a Sherlock Holmes style sleuth perusing the information through his extra-large magnifying glass is as welcome as a quick spin in the dentist's chair.

These slide shows (decks) usually consist of 114 pages, all filled to the brim with tepid data, spoon fed to audiences in the usual 'read your bullets out loud' style.

This kind of torture is along the same lines as your neighbours coming home after 3 weeks on the Algarve, armed with numerous video tapes, loaded with sight-seeing adventures and local attractions, and ready to deliver for you a 'thrill filled' evening of wrist slitting dreariness.

Presentations that bleat on and on without a much needed crisp edit of salient facts, intertwined with anecdotal evidence and stories, is sadly the norm and it's time we changed this, for good.

I had the unfortunate 'pleasure' of sitting through an introductory presentation that promised to be a 5 minute summary of existing business headlines, and became a stumbling 45 minute ramble which lost the audience so completely that they were reading, texting, even snoring, in fact anything rather than paying attention to the information that was being laboured through by the totally unaware presenter.

A colleague of mine in America takes work with him into every *PowerPoint*presentation he has to attend so as to ensure he is not totally wasting his time!

Frankenstein

Sometimes a monster is born and becomes a menace that is hard to control. Usually this monster is our creation (with a little help from our friends) and even we can't control it.

I'm talking about those presentations that are cobbled together using a number of other people's offerings and a few slides we may stumble upon online.

In the earlier chapter in which we discussed planning your winning presentation we advised you to 'Mind the Gap' so you could build

116

your communication in a way that is focused on your goals and will talk directly to your audience.

The **Frankenstein** presentation, which consists of some slides you used a year ago (updated maybe) some slides from a colleague who has presented on a similar subject recently, and some slides you found on a presentation sharing website, ignores the **GAP** process, and is incredibly difficult to control.

You end up with just a slide show rather than a performance that delivers true value to your listeners.

Whenever I have seen these *Frankenstein's* in action, I rarely see an engaged and hooked in audience.

I'll do it on the night...

Sadly there are so many opportunities thrown away due to a lack of preparation, a lack of practice, and a lack of care, and so much of our time wasted by the presenter who decides it will be ok to 'busk it'.

On most of my training courses, I expect each of my delegates to present a number of times. I find this the best way to reaffirm the key lessons learned,andit makes their training extremely real and focused. Everyone comes armed with a presentation, sometimes as short as a 5 minute show, and we work on these during the course to develop our skills.

Before we begin, I ask each attendee to present their piece so I can establish how confident they are, their style, the strengths and weaknesses that we can focus on, and to also give them a reference point to see how dramatic the difference is once they have passed through the training.

I have a very relaxed style to my training and this helps to relax our somewhat nervous presenters as they stand up for the first time to give us their magic. I usually ask a few questions before they begin, such as 'what is the presentation about?', 'how long did it take?' and 'have you rehearsed?

You would imagine that anyone coming on to a presentation training course that requires you to present your own material would at least have a run through of their stuff before attending – and fortunately most do. However, too many admit to running through their content in **their heads only,** and this produces an outcome so common that I can put it into the following equation:

5 minute presentation rehearsed in head only=

10 minute presentation spoken outloud =

*overrun = **problem***

Why oh why do we not rehearse, out loud, in front of a mirror, or even better, in front of colleagues, friends and family, or even pets?

It makes such a difference, it makes such a difference, it makes such a difference, IT MAKES SUCH A DIFFERENCE.

Clearly, I can't emphasise that enough. Your rehearsal, *will* streamline your performance. It willallow you to edit and re-work your show and ensure you are on time, and on message, and will decrease your nervousness exponentially (as we saw in the earlier chapter).

You can spot them a mile off – those presentations that have not been rehearsed (out loud) and sadly, these are the ones that are the biggest waste of everyone's time.

You wouldn't expect a magician to arrive on stage and simply *'have a go'* at some tricks he has seen. Each and every part of their performance is perfected to the smallest degree. Similarly, you would not be in safe hands if your doctor approached a procedure with a cheery *'let's give this a go and see what happens'* attitude; fortunately, the training and practice required for this vocation is more stringent than that.

It's not much to ask, and it continues to amaze me how numerous professional business people expect to be able to deliver their best work to an expectant audience without even a practice and a warm up. Incredible, and if this is you, I implore you will try a rehearsal for size and see what an incredible difference it can make.

Summary Chapter 15 – What not to do...

Bullet laden *PowerPoint* slides, read to an audience do not make for communication that wins. Borrowed slides and poor preparation will let you down again and again and again.

At best, these type of shows deliver some snippets of useful detail that can be used by the audience. Typically, however, they bore the pants off those unfortunate enough to have to attend.

Avoid this massive waste of everybody's time, put yourself in the audience's shoes – shake it up and deliver something different and inspiring. You can, and you must do better than all of these heart-breaking, mind-numbing and unwanted slide shows.

16. **Hand Outs**

There is a big difference between the trusty Hand Out and a set of presentation notes.

How many times has a presenter arrived and distributed their notes (usually in the form of a print off of his *PowerPoint* slides) and then proceeded to run through everything you have in front of you adding nothing along the way?

If you are inquisitive, like most of us, you have read through the content before the presenter has even warmed up, and if you read slowly, like me, the opening of the presentation is a blur because we are still reading the slide show notes instead of concentrating on the delivery by the 'professional'.

How many times has a presenter arrived, distributed their notes (*PowerPoint* slides) and then turned on their heel and walked out of the door, never to be seen again?

Sadly, I have never experienced this, but I wish I had, many, many times in the past. What a mountain of time this would save and we would not have to sit through an experience which we already have the script for (including 'notes to self' "pause while audience laugh" etc.).

So what should we do?

Hand outs are a fabulous resource if you are delving into technical or complicated waters and need some supporting material which is too complex or lengthy to physically present from the stage.

Any material which is essential but requires considered thought, digestion, and reflection, is best delivered in the 'pizza box' of the hand out.

As a rule of thumb, if it is going to make your audience yawn, then put it in your hand out. Incidentally, if you want your audience to actually read your hand outs, please keep those yawns down to an absolute minimum. Who wants to read tedious information? Who does actually read it? It's about time we changed the expectations of audiences everywhere and gave them something that will make them miss a beat – let's shake things up and talk to people in a way that works.

If you want to circulate a set of 'fit for purpose' presentation notes in the form of a hand out, then consider taking the information straight from your note cards (with added detail to put the information into perspective). This way your audience will hear 'your' voice which is what they want, hence attending your presentation.

The Notes View in *PowerPoint* is useful here as this is a resource that will more accurately reflect upon your words and sentiment, as well as give your audience a more human breakdown of what you have been presenting to them.

Whoa there – not yet...

It is quite common to be given presentation notes and hand outs before the presentation begins – I can see this would make sense as it prevents people taking notes (potentially) so they can concentrate on your words as you deliver them. However, in practice, whatever you give to your audience will provide a distraction throughout your show rather than an aide memoir for after the action.

There is a reason sales people do not give their clients brochures during the sell stage of their meetings (unless, of course they are using them as a distraction technique – useful from a body language perspective sometimes).

Save your hand outs for the end of your presentation, by all means refer to them if you want to dissuade your audience from making notes, but don't give them anything that will provide a diversion from your impact.

Don't forget how important the opening of your presentation is – the laborious passing along of printed pages is hardly the highest impact of starts is it?

I like to promise my audience something exciting at the end of my show and the hand outs (if appropriate) have more of a 'gift' feel to them. Entice your audience into your hand out area, promise treats and additional value – step this way Hansel & Gretel I have something for you...

Summary Chapter 16 – Hand outs

There is usually a big difference between information that deserves to be included in a hand out and the detail that is physically presented during your show.

If you are providing hand outs then give your audience a treat and actually make them worth reading. Add additional value, more key detail and bonus material.

Think of your hand out as a gift for all of those who have enjoyed your show. This way, you are far more likely to construct something that will be a worthy accompaniment to your magic. ☐

17. **The Golden Rules**

During my *Invisible PowerPoint* show, I reveal a simple set of rules to enhance the power, focus, and impact of every presentation you will ever make – and all this in 30 - 60 minutes – amazing stuff indeed, and some would say 'life changing' (well one person did but that will do me).

So let's have a look at these simple steps which will ensure your communication is everything your audience requires and a little more.

1.   You are your presentation and not your slides

Typically, far too much emphasis is placed on the visual part of the show – I am talking about *PowerPoint* slides, flip chart creations, and video segments.   Your audience have attended your presentation to hear YOU, to learn from YOUR knowledge, so give them the real article, share what you know and engage your audience personally. If you rely on your slides to tell your story you will lose your audience 9 times out of 10.

You have the power to make a difference – how often have you heard that said about a *PowerPoint* slide?   Make sure the presentation star is you and not your technology.

2.   Create your story first before thinking about *PowerPoint*

Don't forget to 'Mind the GAP' when creating your presentations (see chapter 4 – as if you need reminding). Consider the goals you want to achieve for the audience and for yourself. Who are your audience, what motivates them, how can we get inside their heads? Build your story around these insights and have anecdotes at the ready to reinforce your main points.

I like to create my story in a 'mind map' style (spider diagram) to enable each of my main points to grow and permeate throughout my presentation, and I find it really helpful to have reminders of who my audience are and what I am looking to achieve close at hand throughout this process.

3.   Can the slide do a better job than me? If so how?

Our TV age demands some visual signposts to assist our audience on their learning journey. Remember that *PowerPoint* is one of many visual aids at our disposal, and if we are using slides, that they deliver a more powerful message than can be delivered by us (the human part of the show).

Sometimes a powerful visual, be it a *PowerPoint* slide or a projected image and quotation, are exactly what the moment calls for. If you can truthfully say that your visual delivers more of an impact and a clearer message than you can, then go for it and wow the crowd with your visual magic.

At no point will we allow ourselves to rely wholeheartedly on the visuals, as we know our story is exactly that, **ours**, and the power of delivery is our right, but on occasion a knockout visual will work wonders.

4. Slides are for the audience, not the presenter

It's not rocket science, which is handy, as I know very little about rockets, but so many presenters commit this sin again and again.

We must ensure that all of our slides (visuals) benefit the audience rather than distract them. *PowerPoint* is only one half of our double act and the content of our slides must be designed around our audience's needs only.

Far too often you will find a presenter works from their slides rather than their note cards. I hear it all the time in my training courses;

"I put my information into bullet points to make sure I don't forget anything."

Or

"My slides have everything I need and they keep me on track."

This is a recipe for 'slide reading' rather than presenting – if this is all you have then give me a copy of the slides, in fact email them to me, and I will read them in my own time. That would be much better use of my time; I can read as well as the next man, so bring it on – simple.

How often have you been asked to come along and do a 'slide reading'? How many board rooms do you think we could fill if we advertised our latest information and thoughts about company strategy delivered in a scintillating 45 minute 'slide read'?

Presentations are not about dumping information onto an audience and making for the exit at the earliest opportunity, they are a chance to effect change, to inspire, to take your audience on an amazing journey, and give them something of incredible value.

If you are going to use visuals, and I suggest that you do (but only the ones that add value) then make sure that they are delivering worth directly to your audience – if they don't add flavour and spice to your banquet, then don't put them on the table.

5.   Less is So Much More

It doesn't come much simpler than this.   So much of the presentation magic and communication gold that you are capable of is common sense. We have all been in an audience and we know what works for us, so apply the same rules to your presentations. Put yourselves in the audience's shoes and take a walk around and see how it feels to be them. Ask yourself if your eager throng need all of this information or could you possibly reduce, reduce, reduce to make the sauce that much more memorable and tasty.

Try to creatively edit the content of your slides for added power and a more striking presentation. Your audience have a limited capacity and will remember more of what you do and how you sound than bullets on a slide.

Don't feel that you need to overload your listeners – bite sized gems of information delivered in an extremely digestible format will give extreme satisfaction. You may even find you can give your audience the greatest gift of all – the gift of time. If you can deliver your message with power and impact in half the scheduled time then do it. It may shock a few people along the way (even better) but you will be asked to present again and again, and you will be communicating to win which is not only rare, but also amazing.

6.   You never need to apologise

This sounds a little strange I know, especially to our British audience, as we are ever ready to lay on the apology and undermine ourselves.

I wonder why it is that we feel the need to point out the stuff that weakens our position.

How often have you been part of these kind of scenarios?...

You have been decorating, you have worked hard all weekend, the job is complete and you are mighty proud of your achievements. You invite the neighbours round to show off your handy work and the reason for the banging and clattering coming through the walls for half the night. The neighbours are impressed as you show them your magic *–'wow it looks great, you must be really pleased?'* – *'why thank you most kindly neighbour, I am pleased, really pleased, oh, apart from this little bit over here, that didn't quite go to plan.'*

Why do we feel the need to say that?

Or… you have bought yourself a new car and you love it, it's just what you have been looking for but as soon as you show it to your mates you immediately feel the need to tell them that it *only* cost £x pounds, almost as though you need to apologise for anything that is extravagant.

Trust me on this one – you don't need to apologise; your audience want you to be a success, to entertain and inform. If you begin your presentation with an apology of any kind, then the expectation of your audience will match your negative start.

Do these sound familiar?

"I'm sorry but I haven't had very long to prepare this…"

"I'm ever so nervous…"

"I'm not sure if this is what you are looking for…"

"This is not my presentation so you are going to have to bear with me…"

Or the worse one I have heard for some time:

"I'm sorry but I'm going to have to bore you with my slide show."

Starts like these make me think we are in for a pretty rough ride, and they simply don't add to the magic, they detract from it.

I am not saying we should be something we are not, and you may be nervous and you may not have had long to prepare your show, but your audience, the ones sitting expectantly thinking 'what's in it for me', do not need to know it – keep it to yourself.

Your audience are on your side (usually) and they want a fabulous performance. Psychologically, the amount they enjoy your show will be hugely dependent upon the impression you give during your powerful opening – if you tell them it's going to be great they will be open to your excellence, if you tell them it's going to be bad, not surprisingly, they will be looking for the exit.

When I introduce my *Invisible PowerPoint* show, I quite happily tell my audiences that it is going to be awesome; you should see the smiles on their faces – now that is positive stuff and all you have to do is to live up to the hype – easy.

Summary Chapter 17 – The golden rules

Six simple rules that accompany my *Invisible PowerPoint* show, go on, treat yourself, read them again.

Don't worry, just the titles will do, there's nothing rocket science about this. Just these few rules will radically alter the impact you have on your audience and will make for a far more enjoyable experience for you and for them.

18. **Power ups**

Living up to a presentation that you introduce as 'awesome', takes a little work, but nothing we can't cope with – it's all pretty straight forward after all, but you need to work at it.

If your preparation is well thought out and fit for purpose, you are comfortable with the direction of your communication and your chosen style of delivery, then you are ready for some 'power ups' to really make your show fly.

A perfect start

As we have established, the opening of your presentation is key, not just because it is the first evidence your audience can analyse to clarify how much use your show will be to them, but also because it sets you up as the professional speaker you are.

Your powerful, 'hooktastic' opening is not just for the audience, but it has got to make you feel good too and set the scene, internally, for your confident and powerful performance.

This being the case, I would suggest you practice your opening extensively, and if in any doubt as to exactly what you are going to say and how it should come across, feel free to write your introduction out in full.

I don't advocate reading word for word from cue cards, or writing masses of notes, as you will be constantly distracted by your pages of words instead of concentrating on your audience, but if there is a point in your presentation where the nerves will be dancing across your mind and your mouth may feel dry as your pulse races, it will be at the start.

If you think that this will ease your tensions, then have your opening written out so you can refer to it as often as you wish to get you on your way.

Just the fact that the words will be in front of you will ease some of the stresses we feel when we are about to embark on a presentation adventure,and once you are up and running, you are far more likely to flow like a pro.

A bear walks into a bar

You know the joke:

A bear walks into a bar and says: barman, can I please have ....a pint of bitter. And the barman says to the bear, 'why the big paws'?

If we are intending on presenting like professionals, then we too should include regular pauses in our show, as these are the unspoken gifts that will make a huge difference to our message.

We mentioned the power of the pause in our chapter about body language, and at that point I promised you something a little *wild*, and here it is. The pause is such a powerful tool, that we should all be using it whenever we communicate – unless we have nothing interesting or important to say, that is.

So the next time you communicate to a group, add regular '**a bear walks into a bar**' moments into your show.

The way this works is you make an important point and then (in your head) you say 'a bear walks into a bar...' which is just enough time for the pause to land within your audience. This will give your listeners the time to digest your message and look up in your direction, and by then you will be smiling because you know the rest of the joke.

Try it out, what's the worst (best) that can happen? Try not to smile too much if your content is rather serious and calls for an understated and grave delivery.

As with all great rules, this one can be broken for dramatic effect. Sometimes you will want to bombard your spectators with a flurry of words delivered in a pulse raising crescendo of noise which carries your audience on a wave of communication and delivers them to your chosen destination, slightly breathless but in fabulous shape.

I thoroughly enjoy those moments during a presentation when the tempo quickens and you are carried along in a 'whoosh' of information, and I regularly build these into my show.

Try it, it is great fun, but try to keep your bursts of verbal energy limited to those moments where you need to crank up the pace to push the message forcefully into the back of the net.

Daddarrr!

Even the word is magical, but the power of the 'daddarr' is even more special.

Have you ever been to a presentation where your host has the audience eating out of their hand? They are hanging on every word as though a spell has been cast. These shows are, unfortunately, far too rare, but if you have been to a communication session that has enthralled you, then you will know what I am talking about.

Chances are, these are the only kinds of presentations that we remember, out of the hundreds that we attend over our lifetime.

If you can entice your audience with your story, then your performance will be truly memorable.

A fabulous way to achieve this 'edge of the seat' communication, is to build the suspense and anticipation before delivering your key messages.

This is something we can all do, and the great story tellers have been doing this for centuries.

Build it up, tease a little, build it up some more, pause, and then **BANG!** Deliver your magic.

Just like with any surprise, the build-up is key. This may take some practice, but it will enhance your delivery and add a little dynamite to your performance.

Imagine you are in the audience and your presenter begins his point with the following words:

"Once in a while, if you are fortunate, you will hear a message that is so profound that it literally takes your breath away. It stops you in your tracks and causes you to think in a new way. Just like the song on the radio that is so pure, and sounds so complete, that you have to stop what you are doing and devote every ounce of your

focus to the music. Well, I have had one such moment recently and I would like to share that with you."

Pause

Daddarr!

Whatever comes next is going to have everyone's attention, they are primed and ready for something that sounds like pure gold, and they will want it real bad.

Ideally you structure your 'tease' so it fits with your 'gold' and doesn't over sell the message that you are about to deliver, but it will pay you dividends to employ some 'building of the suspense' tactics and will engage your eager listeners on a deep and powerful level.

Have a go next time you are communicating to a colleague, have some fun with it and build this tactic into your next *awesome* presentation.

Summary Chapter 18 – Power ups

The potency of your message will be greatly assisted by a professional start. Work especially hard at perfecting the opening minutes to fine tune the impact. If you need to write your opening magic out in full then this is ok in my book (try not to read it word for word) but give yourself all the tools you need to make the right impression.

Regular pauses after your important points will give your audience the time to absorb your messages. The more they sink in, the more success you can expect.

There is nothing like a bit of suspense if the reward is powerful and worth the wait. You can increase the effectiveness of your key messages by building a little tension before revealing your communication gold.

19. Communicating to Win – What Next?

Well, our journey is at an end and I think we have come a long way and covered some fascinating ground.

Once we have absorbed the lessons within these pages and are ready to put them into practice, then communicating to win can really begin – all we need now is an audience.

Just like every other aspect of our lives, the excitement takes many forms and so will your audience.

Opportunities to present to your team, your boss, your employees, your children, your family, a boardroom full of managers, a village hall full of photographers, a bus full of tourists, a church full of believers, a locker room full of hopefuls; to shine in front of an interview panel, to entertain in front of the bride's family, to survive in front of a baying crowd on open mic night, to engage, to challenge, to convince, to inspire, and to transform – whatever the opportunity, you need to embrace it with both hands and go for it.

I currently have the honour of creating and delivering a Best Man's speech for my mate Andy, and even though I have presented and spoken in front of a huge variety of audiences, this one will be a first for me.

To be honest, I am a little nervous (always a good sign I believe – it simply means I care enough) but my nerves are outweighed by the excitement I feel to have this enviable opportunity (some would say unenviable but they would be wrong – ask any Best Man once he has finished his speech).

I will approach my speech in the same way as my presentations, with a thorough consideration of who my audience are, what they are looking for, how best to hook them and deliver an entertaining and rewarding experience for all concerned.

My visuals may be a bit more of a challenge but we will see...

What an opportunity, what a varied audience, talk about treading on eggshells,but a superb chanceto put my skills to the test.

I encourage you all to embrace every occasion where your presentation skills can come to the fore, raise your hand, stand tall and look for the moments where there is an audience to be entertained, informed, inspired, and taken on a journey of discovery.

Weekly meetings, club discussions, open forums, debating opportunities, sales pitches, marketing briefs, product reviews, networking evenings, proposals (business and pleasure), birthday parties, engagements, weddings, even funerals; every scenario where your communication could benefit an audience.

You are the future of communication and you have a unique take on the information required – you can be you, and you can and will present like the expert you are.

The adventures are out there, everywhere; go, seek them out, change your world and communicate to win.

A word from Nick

Feet on the Ground Training Ltd work with a huge variety of organisations and individuals. If you have found the content in these pages has resonated with you and you feel that I could help you or your team enhance your communication expertise then please feel free to get in touch.

I can be contacted at the following address:

nick@feetontheground.co.uk

All the best with your communication journey, enjoy.